50 Japanese WHISKIES

TASTED IN JAPAN

50 *Japanese* WHISKIES
TASTED IN JAPAN

Marc Antomattei

MARC ANTOMATTEI PRESS

MARC ANTOMATTEI PRESS

Published by Marc Antomattei Press™
marcantomatteiproductions@gmail.com

Copyright © 2020 by Marc Antomattei
All rights reserved
including the right of reproduction
in whole or in part in any form.
Designed & written by Marc Antomattei
All photography by Marc Antomattei
except all photos of Chichibu Distillery (page 112),
all photos of Suntory Chita Distillery (page 114) are courtesy of
the House of Suntory,
all photos of Nikka Miyagikyo and Yoichi Distilleries (page 122, 126),
all photos of Kavalan (page 160) and Kavalan Distillery (page 162),
photo of Marc Antomattei (page 176) by Mewan Pradeep
are courtesy of their respective copyright owners.

978-0-9846391-4-4 (Hardcover)
978-0-9846391-5-1 (Paperback)
978-0-9846391-6-8 (E-Book)

CONTENTS

V Contents
IX Dedications
01 Preface
05 Glossary
09 How To Use This Guide

THE WHISKIES | ALPHABETIZED (SOMEWHAT) BY MAKER & WHISKY

Page # | Entry #
11 1 Chichibu Ichiro's Malt & Grain World Blended Whisky Limited Edition
13 2 Chichibu Ichiro's Malt & Grain World Blended Whisky White Label
15 3 Chichibu Ichiro's Malt Japanese Pure Malt Whisky Double Distilleries
17 4 Chichibu Ichiro's Malt Pure Malt Whisky MWR Mizunara Wood Reserve
19 5 Chichibu Ichiro's Malt Pure Malt Whisky Wine Wood Reserve
21 6 Chivas Regal Mizunara Special Edition Aged 12 Years
23 7 Eigashima Akashi Red (Blended Whisky)
25 8 Eigashima White Oak Akashi (Blended Whisky)
27 9 Eigashima White Oak Akashi (Single Malt Whisky)
29 10 Eigashima White Oak Akashi Single Malt Aged 8 Years Old Sherry Butt
31 11 Eigashima Sea Front Mellow & Mild
33 12 San Foods Green Forest Rich & Woody
35 13 Toa Shuzo Karugamo Clear & Smooth
37 14 Kirin 2017 Distiller's Select Single Grain
39 15 Kirin 2017 Distiller's Select Single Malt
41 16 Kirin Fuji-Sanroku
43 17 Kirin Fuji-Sanroku Signature Blend
45 18 Kirin Pure Malt Whisky
47 19 Kirin Whiskey Pure & Mellow Riku Land Discovery
49 20 Mars Blended Whisky Saigo Don
51 21 Mars Maltage Cosmo
53 22 Mars Twin Alps
55 23 Misago Blended Whisky in Oak Barrel
57 24 Misago Blended Whisky Bourbon Cask Finish Aged 5 Years
59 25 Nikka Black Nikka Whisky (from the 1980s)
61 26 Nikka Black Nikka Special
63 27 Nikka Black Rich Blend
65 28 Nikka Coffey Grain Whisky

CONTENTS

Page # | Entry #
67 29 Nikka Coffey Malt Whisky
69 30 Nikka Whisky Date
71 31 Nikka Whisky Taketsuru Pure Malt
73 32 Nikka Whisky Taketsuru Pure Malt Aged 12 Years
75 33 Nikka Whisky Taketsuru Pure Malt Aged 17 Years
77 34 Nikka The Nikka 12 Years Old
79 35 Nikka Whisky Single Malt Miyagikyo
81 36 Nikka Whisky Single Malt Yoichi
83 37 Nikka Whisky Super
85 38 Suntory The Chita
87 39 Suntory The Hakushu Distiller's Reserve
89 40 Suntory Hibiki Japanese Harmony
91 41 Suntory Hibiki Blender's Choice
93 42 Suntory Kakubin
95 43 Suntory Whisky Royal Blended Whisky
97 44 Suntory Torys Classic
99 45 Suntory Torys Extra Honey
101 46 Suntory World Whisky AO
103 47 Suntory Yamazaki Distillery Single Malt Whisky (Distillery Only)
105 48 Suntory The Yamazaki Distiller's Reserve
107 49 Suntory The Yamazaki Aged 12 Years
109 50 Suntory The Yamazaki Aged 18 Years

THE DISTILLERIES

113 Chichibu (Saitama)
115 Chita (Aichi)
117 Eigashima formerly White Oak (Hyogo)
119 Fuji Gotemba (Shizuoka)
121 Hakushu (Yamanashi)
123 Miyagikyo (Miyagi)
125 Yamazaki (Osaka)
127 Yoichi (Hokkaido)

CONTENTS

THE BARS

Page #
131 82 Ale House (Tokyo)
133 Apollo (Chiba)
135 The Arty's Bar / Mojito Laboratory (Tokyo)
137 Bar Memphis (Chiba)
139 Bar UK (Osaka)
141 Cabin Nakameguro (Tokyo)
143 One Shot Bar Keith (Osaka)
145 Starbucks Reserve Roastery (Tokyo)
147 Tokyo Whisky Library (Tokyo)

THE BOOKS

151 Japanese Whisky
153 The Way of Whisky
155 Whisky Japan
157 Whisky Rising

HONORARY MENTION

161 [Whisky] Kavalan Classic Single Malt Whisky
163 [Distillery] King Car Kavalan (Taiwan)
165 [Bar] Backyard (Tokyo)
167 [Bar] Brandy Library (New York City)

CLOSING

169 Bibliography
177 About The Author
179 Epilogue

Yumi Yoshikawa from Chichibu Distillery.

Dedication

I thank God for blessing me with the talent of writing. To Eiji-san of Bar UK, a gentleman, and owner of Japan's best bar. My best friend, David Gregory, who gives me the motivation and encouragement to write. My father, who always tells me he loves and supports me no matter what it is I tell him I'm going to do. To my son Michelangelo, I dedicate my works to you. And to my friend Kenny who quoted me and gave me the trademark phrase, "smooth finish."

For their assistance, a special thanks to

Taro Kaneko, Deputy Manager & Brand Ambassador, Asahi Breweries, Ltd.

Yumi Yoshikawa, Brand Ambassador, Venture Whisky Ltd.

Kaitlyn Tsai, Brand Ambassador & Global PR Officer, Kavalan

Yusuke Sasaki, Global Public Relations Department, Suntory Holdings Limited

My whisky tasting notes from handwritten to print to digital.

Preface

PREFACE

"Every whisky has a story."
-Marc Antomattei

Before we get into anything, first let me say this is the most essential notice I can give to readers of my book. Don't let me make any determinations for you. This book may or may not influence your whisky purchasing decisions, but everything here in these pages are my assessments according to my own personal taste and likings. You may agree with me on everything, or you may agree with me on 80 to 90% of my tastings. You may only agree with half of them, or quite possibly, you may love absolutely everything I hate and hate everything I love. That's OK with me. These suggestions I will make in these reviews may not suit everyone's palate.

We all grow up in different regions of the world, and we are subjected to different taste palates and diets. I'm from the United States, the land of the fat and the home of the sweet. We don't as a collective whole even eat half as healthy as Japanese people do. While I have lived in Japan for the past 17 years and have become accustomed to their food, I like my own country's food offerings better. I appreciate the healthy, natural, and organic makeup of Japanese cuisine. Still, taste-wise, it's not the end all be all for food. Not to say I don't like Japanese food, again I just like my food more. Trying to keep this short now, buy what you want.

I may mention in this book some tasting notes along the lines of, "This whisky is a little too spicy or peaty for my liking." Just for example (although I do like peat and spice). Depending on how much I express after that, I may be stressing with emphasis that I dislike it a lot, or maybe just a little. Either way, I'm showing that I

PREFACE

have at least some disdain for it. Now you may personally like spice, you may like peat. You know yourself, and you read into that, and you take that with a grain a salt, because that may be your cue to say to yourself, "OK, I need to go out and buy this whisky immediately." So that's how that works. Just don't hate me because I love differently from you.

More about this book. Even though this is a review book, an index, a databank, and a reference book, I wanted to make a "real book" that you could read cover-to-cover and find interesting stories in. Along with facts included to hold your interest. Just the typical whisky specifications with bullet points would not do. I hope that as a reader, this is something you can truly appreciate as I poured much effort (no pun intended), research, and money into it. Every whisky featured in this book is one I drank personally, with me actually buying bottles and drinking at a bar to an equal extent. Hopefully, the secret that'll keep you reading all the way through is that every whisky has a story. The scale of these stories may vary; some might be grand, others minor. They'll either be stories about events I experienced personally with a whisky, or a story about a particular whisky, maybe involving its history.

There have been four major book releases on the subject matter of Japanese whisky, and for the most part, they are all hitting the same beats but with different wording. A history of Japanese whisky, how Japanese whisky is made, a look at whisky cocktails, a showcase of all the major distilleries, short reviews, etc. The word for this would be double-dipping. What warrants one to write a book if they can't do it either different or better than the last guy? I congratulate Dominic Roskrow for being the first. What sets my book apart from the handful of others who have written on the topic? Well, I'm here boots on the ground, buying and trying this stuff on my own dime.

PREFACE

It's one thing to write about Japanese whisky, get photos sourced from the distillers, collect someone else's reviews, and collage together a book. It is another thing to actually drink and experience everything that you write about for yourself. I've been to these distilleries and bars, I've had everything I wrote about. I've got the receipts and the photographic evidence to back me up.

I'm the sole visionary of my book, and I'm giving you the Steve Jobs experience of what I think a whisky book should be. I'm focused on the consumer experience showcasing the drinks that you are interested in buying. Even if you never knew before about a particular bottle, you may have never known you wanted it. However, after reading an entry on it in my book, it'll entice you to go out and get it. I'm showing you what you want even before you know. My book is about whisky through and through, and putting them front and center. I do humble myself, and I hope you appreciate my efforts in what I'm trying to do.

Kanpai!

Marc Antomattei

MARC T. ANTOMATTEI, Founder, MAP
Author, *50 Japanese Whiskies*

Glossary

GLOSSARY

age statement whisky - a whisky that shows on the bottling label the youngest year component whisky contained in the bottle.

blended whisky - the product of mixing two or more different whiskies, be it of the same grain or different grains.

cask - a large, hollow, cylindrical barrellike container made of wooden staves and bound by wood or metal hoops to store and mature whisky.

cask strength - a whisky bottled at the same strength it came out of the barrel at with no additional water added for dilution. Usually very high in ABV.

chill-filtration - a method of cosmetically removing a cloudy residue from whisky before it is bottled. A non-chill filtered whisky when chilled, or with the addition of ice or water, naturally produces a haze that some drinkers may find undesirable. Removing this haze does not affect the taste whatsoever.

column still - a piece of distillation equipment made of either copper or stainless steel for continuous distillation.

distillation - the process of separating alcohol from fermented liquid and eliminating the residue of the yeast and unfermentable matter.

dram - a single-shot serving of whisky.

grain whisky - whisky made mostly from corn, wheat or rye, and hardly any malted barley.

GLOSSARY

maturation - the process of letting whisky sit in a wooden barrel in a warehouse to mature. It is vital to the taste, aromas, and natural coloring of a whisky.

malt - dried, germinated cereal grain.

malt whisky - whisky made from a fermented mash consisting mostly of malted barley.

mizunara - Japanese oak wood.

no age statement - acronym NAS, is a whisky without an age (how many years it matured in a barrel) written on the bottle label.

peat - a soil-like layer of earth below topsoil that consist of partly decomposed vegetable matter. It is cut, dried, and burnt in a fire with dry malted barely over it, absorbing the smoke. The process makes a smoky aromatic and tasting whisky with a character described as peaty.

pot still - a piece of distillation equipment usually made of copper in a wide array of shapes and sizes for batch distillation. It's used to distill mainly water and alcohol along with other components to make a high ABV spirit.

pure malt - the result of blending two or more different types of single malt whiskies from different distilleries. The term is archaic, albeit still used in Japan to describe a blended malt whisky.

sherry - a fortified wine made from white grapes grown in the south of Spain in Andalusia. Some whisky is matured or finished in casks that once held sherry wine prior.

HOW TO USE THIS GUIDE
DISTILLERY NAME FOLLOWED BY THE NAME OF JAPANESE WHISKY

Not all, but a lot of my whisky entries will begin with a captain's log. This is an homage to the episodic, cult classic TV show *Star Trek* from the mid to late 1960s. You will notice I will begin most entries with the phrase, "Captain's Log, Stardate" followed by the year, month, and day written in the YYYY.MM.DD format. The acting captain of the starship in this show always made this record, a voice recorded log entry of the current status of a mission. The date I write in my captain's log is clearly the date I both had and wrote about a whisky.

The format and layout, while not the same, are lightly inspired by the city reference Michelin guides that rank restaurants and hotels in metropolitan cities. In terms of voice, our books couldn't be any more different. The *Michelin Guide* entries are written in a neutral but serious tone, my book's tone is very friendly. I'm providing easy-to-read information in a familiar voice for casual (general knowledge) drinkers, aficionados, and experts. Everyone, regardless of their overall knowledge level, will be able to take something from my writings, albeit some more than others.

- **Nose:** The aroma of a whisky experienced through sniffing.
- **Palate:** The taste of a whisky while held in the mouth.
- **Finish:** The aftertaste remaining in the mouth after swallowing.
- **Color:** Only official distiller assessed whisky colors will be listed.
- **ABV:** Alcohol by volume, the strength at which a whisky is bottled at indicating the alcohol/water mixture level.
- **Distillery:** Name of the distillery from which a whisky derives.
- **Price:** The retail, online, or auction price of a whisky intra-Japan shown only in Japanese yen ¥ (bottle size listed in milliliters).

Whisky entry number → #00

CHICHIBU ICHIRO'S MALT & GRAIN WORLD BLENDED WHISKY LIMITED EDITION

Captain's Log, Stardate 2018.11.25. This is it! The very first entry of my first whisky book. Kicking off things with a good one here, and a story, a method of writing I will employ in many entries starting now. Every whisky has a story, whether it's its own, or my experience with it.

I attended the Whisky Festival 2018 in Tokyo for the first time this year. It's actually the first I've heard of this event even though it's been going on annually for 11 years. Incidentally, and coincidentally I found out that it started in 2007 via the Chichibu Distillery. They released a limited edition Japanese single malt whisky bottling at last year's event called none other than the Whisky Festival 10th Anniversary.

So I'm at this event and Chichibu has a full lineup at their table of all their latest and greatest hits, everything is available to try. The first drink of the event I delved into was this Limited Edition blended whisky. This is made mainly with over 10-year-old Chichibu stock. You can detail and smell the grains in this one quite easily as it features a sweet cereal aroma. A very nice dram, but I couldn't tell you which I like better between it and the standard Ichiro's World Blended Whisky White Label. Try both.

- **Nose:** Sweet cereal, maple syrup, and vanilla.
- **Palate:** Light spicy kick. Maple and vanilla cream sweetness.
- **Finish:** Chewable.
- **ABV:** 48%.
- **Distillery:** Chichibu. Old Hanyu Distillery stock was used for the first few batches but isn't anymore.
- **Price:** Approximately ¥20,000 online intra-Japan (700ml).

#01

CHICHIBU ICHIRO'S MALT & GRAIN WORLD BLENDED WHISKY WHITE LABEL

Captain's Log, Stardate 2017.10.10. It was the third anniversary party of one of the best bars in the Greater Tokyo Area, Bar Memphis in Inage, Chiba, Japan. It's always the owner Nao and the music playing in the background that really sets the atmosphere of the place and makes it lively. On any given night, you could be hearing blues, soul, or jazz music. I was at the party celebrating with everyone else, but I was also looking for something very Japanese. I wanted something that either I didn't already own or have ever tried before. Then I found this whisky.

This is a non-chill filtered, non-colored, NAS blended whisky from an independent distillery by the name of Chichibu owned by Ichiro Akuto (hence the name of the whisky Ichiro's). It's made from distillate from Japan, Scotland, Ireland, the United States, and Canada.

As a NAS, it reminds me of something I tried before but can't quite necessarily place my finger on. I think this whisky is just a little bit better than an average affair. The aftertaste is the best part; it stayed with me long after my final sip. On pricing, obviously, this cost more in other regions of the world, about double, but in Japan, it is rather affordable.

- **Nose:** Ethanol. Adding water helped me suppress that and brought out an airy and sweet peachy smell. After an extended nosing, I realized this smells very much the same as how Malibu Coke taste, that being Malibu rum liqueur and Coca-Cola.
- **Palate:** Rich in vanilla like a vanilla Coke. Nutty.
- **Finish:** Everlasting.
- **ABV:** 46.5%.
- **Distillery:** Chichibu. The first few batches include Hanyu stock.
- **Price:** ¥4,180 tax included (700ml).

#02

CHICHIBU ICHIRO'S MALT JAPANESE PURE MALT WHISKY DOUBLE DISTILLERIES (GREEN LABEL)

Captain's Log, Stardate 2018.11.12. Before heading over to the Tokyo Whisky Library for the very first time this same night, I went to the Tokyo ward of Meguro to visit my Brazilian friend Sullivan Gouvea. He is the head bartender over at CABIN Naka-Meguro, a posh and cozy spirits bar located in an upscale neighborhood of Central Tokyo. I met this guy over a decade ago when we both resided in Yokohama, the neighboring city of Tokyo. We were practicing Brazilian jiu-jitsu together at the same dojo at that time.

So I was looking for a whisky that I never had before, something new and Japanese. It was Sullivan's recommendation I try this, a pure malt made by blending two single malts from two distilleries. Arguably it was the best-blended whisky I had all year. Like many other Chichibu releases, this also is a non-chill-filtered, non-colored release. Sullivan told me the price is slowly creeping up on this one. He and others believe it will be discontinued soon because it is the last of the old stock. It comes from Ichiro Akuto's grandfather and then the father's now-defunct Hanyu Distillery. At the 2018 Tokyo Whisky Festival, I asked a representative about this very thing. They expressed to me that even though Hanyu is now demolished, they still have stock, and they still want to release it and wish to continue to make it.

- **Nose:** Sweet vanilla, citrus fruits.
- **Palate:** Spicy smooth (when no water is added), moderate citrus oranges come up but it's playful like sherbet candy.
- **Finish:** Creamy vanilla, lingering.
- **ABV:** 46%.
- **Distillery:** Chichibu & Hanyu. The current batch is mainly Chichibu.
- **Price:** Approximately ¥17,000 online intra-Japan (700ml).

#03

CHICHIBU ICHIRO'S MALT PURE MALT WHISKY MWR MIZUNARA WOOD RESERVE (GOLD LEAF LABEL)

Captain's Log, Stardate 2018.11.12. So I went to the Tokyo Whisky Library on this night, anticipating finding a new base of operations for my whisky consumption for both business and personal pleasure. When expectations are set as high as mine were, you're bound to be let down. It was such an underwhelming experience. I was expecting Brandy Library (as in the famed NYC bar) 2, but it didn't hold up to those standards set up by the place that came on the scene a decade before. More on that in my bar review of the Tokyo Whisky Library.

As standard with most, if not all of Ichiro's whiskies, it's non-chill filtered and non-colored. It's a passable drink, not the strongest in Chichibu's armory. It depends on how much you can buy your bottle or bar dram for. For the right price, it would have made for a decent daily dram. For what I paid (¥1,800) at the bar and for what's being charged for it online, you'd probably feel cheated.

By the way, don't let the name fool you. Even though the words Pure Malt are in the title, this is not a single malt. It's instead a blended whisky made up of many malt whiskies (no grains) blended together. These malts come from both the Chichibu Distillery and the now-defunct Hanyu Distillery.

- **Nose:** Oaky, a little ethanol and medical like. Smokier than the other Ichiros I've had, which were not smoky in the least bit.
- **Palate:** Light smoke, spicy oak.
- **Finish:** Light smoke and spice.
- **ABV:** 46%.
- **Distillery:** Chichibu & Hanyu. The current batch is mainly Chichibu.
- **Price:** Approximately ¥13,000 online intra-Japan (700ml).

#04

CHICHIBU ICHIRO'S MALT PURE MALT WHISKY WINE WOOD RESERVE (RED LEAF LABEL)

Made with malt from French oak ex-red wine barrels. Like the other leaf label bottlings from Chichibu distillery, this is bottled at the same strength as those without added coloring and non-filtered. Like the other leaf label bottlings, this is a blended malt (called pure malt in Japan). Part of it comes from the now-defunct Hanyu distillery, owned and managed previously by Ichiro Akuto's father Yutaka. Hanyu was closed down in the year 2000 because of a recession in the economy.

While I personally didn't pull any vinous aromas away from this, I could definitely taste a vinous taste on the palate and in the finish. It wasn't so subtle that you can barely taste it, on the contrary, it was heavy enough to find even without trying to.

Chichibu really makes some good stuff and is such a respectable and reputable maker of whisky. Variety is the word I'm looking for to explain their releases. Not any two of them are the same, and you can really differentiate between them quite easily. But just as their popularity goes up, so does their prices, and I'm not too happy about that.

- **Nose:** Medicinal like, heavy smell, and oaky. I'm not a wine specialist, so you may or may not find a wine aroma in there.
- **Palate:** Light spice, red wine, sherry, berries and cherries.
- **Finish:** Chewable finish with fruity berries, wine.
- **ABV:** 46%.
- **Distillery:** Chichibu & Hanyu. The current batch is mainly Chichibu.
- **Price:** ¥12,500- online intra-Japan (700ml).

#05

CHIVAS REGAL MIZUNARA SPECIAL EDITION AGED 12 YEARS BLENDED SCOTCH WHISKY

In June 2018, I bought a bottle of this at Bic Camera in Namba, Osaka, an electronic store of 7 floors that carries everything (yes, even alcohol). I bought the half-size bottle in the case if I have hated it, I wouldn't have spent a lot of money on it and then tried to figure out what to do with the rest.

This isn't a Japanese whisky per se. This is a Scottish whisky from world-renowned master blender Colin Scott inspired by Japanese whiskies. The bottle's front label says it "has been created especially for the discerning Japanese whisky enthusiast." For this, "carefully selected malt whisky and grain whisky are married and finished in rare mizunara (Japanese oak) casks in Japan." A date can also be found on the front of the label, I believe it to be the date and time of bottling.

I'm not sure if this is available outside of Japan, for it only appears on the Japanese Chivas website. I wouldn't change anything about it, as it is so well balanced, and such a good attempt at making a Japanese-style whisky. You can tell it was meticulously prepared, and I highly recommend to fans of Japanese whisky and Speysides. With those Scots being the masters of whisky, I'm not surprised at them pulling this off.

- **Nose:** Sweet oranges, toffee. Light vanilla detected after the first sip during second nosing.
- **Palate:** Gentle on the tongue, buttery and smooth, bright oranges, extremely light peat/smoke.
- **Finish:** Smooth, extremely light smoke, memorable aftertaste.
- **Color:** Warm amber.
- **ABV:** 40%.
- **Distillery:** Strathisla.
- **Price:** ¥3,564 tax included (700ml).

#06

EIGASHIMA AKASHI RED BLENDED WHISKY

The Eigashima Distillery owned by Eigashima Shuzo Co. Ltd. acquired their whisky manufacturing license in year 8 (1919) of the Taishō period (aka Taishō era). They are the first to obtain a permit to make whisky according to their website. To explain the Taishō period, it is a period in Japanese history spanning from July 30, 1912, to December 25, 1926, coinciding with the rule of the Emperor, Yoshihito. He was simply called Emperor during his life rule of Japan and posthumously known as Emperor Taishō.

You can read more about the distillery in the back of the book. I feel conflicted about some made claims from their website.

Akashi Red is the entry-level blended whisky of malt and grain from the Eigashima Distillery. "Akashi Red is a blended whisky reserved in Japanese Shochu cask (American Oak) for 3 years, aged in ex-bourbon casks before finishing in ex-sherry casks for 2 years."
–Toki No Sakagura

The whisky comes in only one bottle size offering, which is 500ml. This is quite possibly the cheapest, decent whisky you can pick up in Japan. While I found a few other whiskies that are cheaper (e.g., Top Value Whisky), they really aren't worth your time.

- **Nose:** A light fruity smell, a hint of chocolate.
- **Palate:** Sharp apples.
- **Finish:** The finish is the highpoint of this whisky. It's after you swallow that first gulp does that fruity taste truly make its impact. Light chocolate.
- **ABV:** 40%.
- **Distillery:** Eigashima formerly White Oak.
- **Price:** ¥770 before tax (500ml).

#07

EIGASHIMA WHITE OAK AKASHI BLENDED WHISKY

This is one of the cheaper and better Japanese whiskies available, and the first Akashi, aka White Oak whisky I've ever tried. I heard about it from a Forbes contributor article* titled "10 Japanese Whiskies to Try Now," written by Karla Alindahao. It was not so much Karla's writing that made me want to pick up this bottle (maybe I got no influence from the article whatsoever). It was rather how refreshing the whisky looked in the picture, sitting in its container. It looked like liquid gold in a nicely shaped bottle to me.

This is from the Eigashima Distillery, formerly known as the White Oak Whisky Distillery in Akashi City, Hyogo Prefecture just west of and bordering Kobe city, Japan. This is a Scotch type blended whisky "reserved in Japanese Shochu cask (American Oak) for 3 years, aged in ex-bourbon casks before finishing in ex-sherry casks for 2 years." -Toki No Sakagura

Captain's Log, Supplemental 2020.3.4. After having this again, after some years, I realize this whisky seems very insubstantial. Elaborating on that, I mean it's very light and tastes young. I'm not saying it's terrible, just immature. It's still a go in my book, figuratively and literally.

- **Nose:** Smells like light ethanol. Leaves a whole lot to be desired.
- **Palate:** Toffee.
- **Finish:** Strong and vibrant toffee that hits with a more intense flavor than that which was found on the palate.
- **Color:** Warm amber gold.
- **ABV:** 40%.
- **Distillery:** Eigashima formerly White Oak.
- **Price:** ¥980 before tax (500ml).

#08

EIGASHIMA WHITE OAK AKASHI SINGLE MALT WHISKY

This is from the Eigashima Distillery in Akashi City, which opened in 1984. Located in Hyogo Prefecture just west of and bordering Kobe city Japan. The original Eigashima Distillery was established to make sake and shochu but later started producing whisky. Founding company Eigashima Shuzo Co. Ltd. obtained a license to start producing whisky back in 1919. Even though it was the first (or one of the first?) to get the license, I don't think it was distilling whisky back at that time. So are they indeed the earliest producers of Japanese whisky? That's a rhetorical question. Having a license and no product doesn't make it so.

This non-chill filtered and non-colored whisky appears to be the distillery's number-one and most significant malt. Website www.tokinosakagura.com says, "Akashi NAS Single Malt Whisky is a blend of 7 yr, 5 yr and 4 yr malts, from 3 different types of cask, Spanish Cherry Oak, American Oak and Bourbon Oak casks." This is yet another decent and affordable whisky in Japan.

I procured mine from the Mega Don Quijote in Shibuya. Don Quijote is a Japanese discount chain store that sells everything from groceries to electronics, clothes, etc. It is usually open until the early hours of the morning, and some are 24 hours.

- **Nose:** A little smoky.
- **Palate:** Peat-like smoke.
- **Finish:** Rich, smoky, candy. Goes down easy.
- **Color:** Rich caramel.
- **ABV:** 46%.
- **Distillery:** Eigashima formerly White Oak.
- **Price:** ¥2,916 tax included (500ml).

#09

EIGASHIMA WHITE OAK AKASHI SINGLE MALT WHISKY AGED 8 YEARS OLD SHERRY BUTT #188

The one and only time I made it out to Bar Keith near Shin-Osaka Station, this was one of three whiskies I had at the bar that night. That bar was chock-full of rarities, especially when it came to Akashi whiskies. Make sure you check the bar review in the back of the book but do report back after.

This is one of the best, if not the best, Akashi whisky I've had. Though it's a steep price to try. At the bar, I paid ¥1,400 for a half shot. The only place I could find a bottle priced was at an Australian online retailer called nicks.com.au. It was AU$ 499, but that's long gone. It's non-chill filtered and non-colored (I don't know why that's spelled the British English way on the label, as Japan follows the American standard. But OK). I believe this whisky is cask strength as it is ferociously strong sitting at 55% ABV. You better dilute it with some spoonfuls or droplets of water or risk numbing your taste buds with an alcohol burn. Once you get it right, the taste is beautiful. Heavy sherry, red wine, and apples, oh my!

I mentioned that the bar had a lot of rarities, and this is one of them. On the back label, it is written that this is Bottle No 448/721. That certainly means not that many were produced, and once they're gone, that's it. Get it while you can, if you can.

- **Nose:** Heavy sherry. Red wine with ripe red apples. Toffee and vanilla in the back.
- **Palate:** Sweet and spicy sherry wine. Ripe red apples.
- **Finish:** Smoke-esque spice. It's not really smoke, just more or less the strength you're dealing with.
- **ABV:** 55%.
- **Distillery:** Eigashima formerly White Oak.
- **Price:** N/A. Last known price $AU 499.00 (500ml).

SEA FRONT MELLOW & MILD BLENDED WHISKY

This blended whisky is one of a series of three budget whiskies where each one is made by a different distillery. All of them, though, are licensed and distributed by Mitsubishi Food Co., Ltd. The full set includes Green Forest Rich & Woody by San Foods, Karugamo Clear & Smooth by Toa Shuzo, and this the Sea Front Mellow & Mild by Eigashima, aka White Oak Distillery.

I bought this along with the Green Forest out of the Kohyo grocery store in Osaka, a subsidiary of Aeon supermarket. Sea Front is a reputable offering. Eigashima is one of the most prominent and most recognizable independent production houses in Japan. Known by both Japanese and Western drinkers. To say the least, I expected a lot out of this one.

With how light gold the color is, it tells me this whisky is not colored. It also tells me it is very young (that's very usual from this distillery, young whiskies I mean). I usually put whiskies into a pass or fail list, there's hardly any in-between for me. Although this one is a pass, it barely hits the mark because it's so average and bland. Compared to other Akashi, this is not their best, and it's more expensive than the Akashi Red and White Oak Akashi (Blended Whisky) by about ¥800 to ¥1,000, respectively.

- **Nose:** Wheat grains, bitter, and a bit like whiteboard markers.
- **Palate:** Wheat grains, fruity, dry pears. The intersection of where sweet and bitter meet is here, but they cancel each other out if that makes sense. Dry citrus oranges in the second tasting.
- **Finish:** Pears again. A light bite, but not the kind that'll pucker your face. It features a light, smoke-esque air to it.
- **ABV:** 40%.
- **Distillery:** Eigashima formerly White Oak.
- **Price:** ¥1,814 tax included (500ml).

#11

GREEN FOREST
RICH & WOODY
BLENDED WHISKY

This blended whisky is one of a series of three budget whiskies where each one is made by a different distillery, but all are licensed and distributed by Mitsubishi Food Co., Ltd. The full set includes Sea Front Mellow & Mild by Eigashima, aka White Oak Distillery, Karugamo Clear & Smooth by Toa Shuzo, and this the Green Forest Rich & Woody by San Foods.

San Foods, founded in 1976, is a brewery that makes Japanese sake. The company's home is in Yamanashi, the same prefecture where you can find Mt. Fuji. It is just west of and bordering Tokyo prefecture. They say they "offer high-quality sake at affordable prices." While they have many sakes on the market, this, I believe, is their only whisky. I don't know what this is blended with, as almost any details about it in English or Japanese are practically non-existent online. I can only go off what I find on the back label, and of course, the company website.

Surprising even myself, I have to report I drank a dram of this subsequently right after Sea Front and discovered I'm a little fonder of it. As a NAS, budget whisky, if you approach it without high expectations, you may be pleasantly surprised just as I was.

- **Nose:** Some fumes that smell like a solvent at the beginning that later gives way to a cinnamon smell in the background. There's also a strong potpourri scent that's not sweet but heavy.
- **Palate:** Cinnamon (not spicy), herbal.
- **Finish:** More cinnamon but with no bite.
- **ABV:** 40%.
- **Distillery:** San Foods Co., Ltd.
- **Price:** ¥1,166 tax included (500ml).

#12

KARUGAMO CLEAR & SMOOTH BLENDED WHISKY

Captain's Log, Stardate 2020.6.5. It's crunch time nearing the release of this very book you're reading, and I've had to change this whole review short notice. I was under the impression this was old stock from the defunct Hanyu Distillery. I was made aware by another distillery, the true heirs of Hanyu, that this, in fact, isn't from Hanyu. I was told that the producer of this whisky, Toa Shuzo, just has a Hanyu City address, and it is misinterpreted as being from Hanyu Distillery. The whisky itself is speculated as being bulk whisky from overseas.

As stated in the previous two entries, this whisky is one of a three budget whisky set. Each made by a different distillery, but is distributed by Mitsubishi Food Co., Ltd. While the other two whiskies in this set can still be found in quite a few Japanese supermarkets and liquor stores. This was the hardest whisky in this book for me to track down. I happened upon it at a supermarket in Ichikawa City, Chiba, called Daiei.

Karugamo is a Japanese word meaning Indian spot-billed duck. If you look at the label, you'll see one wearing a red bowtie. The back of the bottle in Japanese says, "Please enjoy this good deep and mild malt with a smooth and light grain in harmony."

- **Nose:** Peaty meets feinty with some grain. It's light peat that smells obscure, yet pleasant.
- **Palate:** Buttery, light smoky peat.
- **Finish:** Buttery smooth, quick smoke release.
- **ABV:** 40%.
- **Distillery:** Toa Shuzo.
- **Price:** ¥2,138 tax included (500ml).

#13

KIRIN 2017 DISTILLER'S SELECT SINGLE GRAIN

I bought this whisky (along with the next entry, the 2017 Distiller's Select Single Malt) on my visit to the Kirin Fuji Gotemba Whisky Distillery on November 7 this same year. They are both limited releases. While I haven't been back to the distillery, I'm sure they probably release this one annually. Most likely, they just slap an updated label on it with the current year.

Although they did have full-size bottles available, I recall them being expensive, and I didn't like much of what I tasted at the distillery bar for a variety of other whiskies. For those reasons, I didn't want to chance it and just bought the 200ml size bottles for both. Both are NAS whiskies with a very light color to them. Whether that color is natural or caramel coloring, I do not know.

The Single Grain had a delightful aroma right from the opening of the screw top. ABV wise it is an intense whisky, so I added some water to dilute it as not to burn my taste buds. If you ever have a chance of picking this one up, don't. This is more of a pass because it's very immature and has no substance to it. The palate is a great part of the experience of drinking whisky, and on the palate, you want instant gratification from the moment it touches your tongue, and this doesn't give that to me.

- **Nose:** Maple with other floral notes.
- **Palate:** It has light grains and faint maple. For a whisky with such strong alcohol content, the taste is just too light. It's almost as if it has no taste at all.
- **Finish:** Surprisingly, even though it was bland on the tongue, it does have a pleasant lingering aftertaste. Buttery smooth.
- **ABV:** 52%.
- **Distillery:** Fuji Gotemba.
- **Price:** ¥2,160 tax included (200ml).

#14

KIRIN 2017 DISTILLER'S SELECT SINGLE MALT

I bought this single malt whisky (along with the previous entry, the 2017 Distiller's Select Single Grain) on my visit to the Kirin Fuji Gotemba Whisky Distillery on November 7, this same year. I think the asking price for both of them was way too much, and I bought the small bottles for both.

This is underwhelming. Neither is this sweet, fruity, floral, peaty, or chocolate. Both whiskies in this limited set are underwhelming, and what I'm going to say next essentially goes for both, not only this. These feel like cheaply made cash grabs. The exclusivity of them, where you can only get them at the distillery will make patrons feel like they have to buy them while there, otherwise, they won't be able to get them again. And then once you get it, you realize you got something with no effort put into making them. They seem immature and aged for the minimum amount of time, to be hurried along and bottled. I don't appreciate this at all.

I'm glad I went through the motions and got to have the experience to taste it just to warn you not to. And hey, the best thing I got out of this was only another entry into my book.

- **Nose:** Some smoke, oak.
- **Palate:** Almost indescribable and not pleasant. Sharp, woody.
- **Finish:** Going down easy is the best thing it has going for itself. A lovely smoky aftertaste.
- **ABV:** 49%.
- **Distillery:** Fuji Gotemba.
- **Price:** ¥2,160 tax included (200ml).

#15

KIRIN FUJI-SANROKU (TARUJUKU 50 DEGREES)

The Kirin story. A lot of people outside of Japan to their knowledge may believe Kirin just to be only a whisky distillery, or a brewery, or both. Actually though for the unknowing, it is, in fact, a beverage company in general. For whisky, this is one of their best.

Unfortunately for fans of this whisky, I got some bad news. Kirin announced they would stop selling it at the end of March 2019 due to a shortage of stock and rising demand. Kirin reported the Fuji-Sanroku made up more than 30% of its whisky sales. Even though it is gone, it has been replaced by its more premium version, the Signature Blend in 2018. Later, the Kirin Whiskey Pure & Mellow Riku Land Discovery in 2020. Again, a little bit unfortunate as for the price/taste, this was the best bang for buck whisky you could possibly buy in Japan. Bar none.

Circa October 2, 2017, the time of my first tasting. At that time, I absolutely loved and adored this whisky. Around one year later, I found it to be not as good as I remember, while the Signature Blend is better than I remember. Time and experience change everything. It's still a good buy and the best bang for buck purchase. Get it while you can.

- **Nose:** Sharp, ethanol, caramel, and maple.
- **Palate:** Sharp in the beginning. Maple, chocolate.
- **Finish:** Smooth. The maple stays with you.
- **ABV:** 50%.
- **Distillery:** Fuji Gotemba.
- **Price:** ¥1,620 tax included (700ml).

#16

KIRIN FUJI-SANROKU SIGNATURE BLEND

Blended by master blender Jota Tanaka, this whisky was offered to me free at the distillery bar after the tour visit to the Fuji Gotemba Distillery on November 7, 2017. In addition to that tasting, I had indeed bought a full-size bottle to take home with me, and I gave it a second analysis there. Meant to be exclusive, you could only purchase this whisky either at the distillery or direct from Kirin by online order. As of my writing of this book review in Osaka on the morning of October 2, 2018. I can say in the past few months I've seen a few of these bottles around town in some liquor shops. Now they are the standard offering at retail, replacing the normal Fuji-Sanroku as of April 2019. This whisky has some similar features as the standard version, which is much beloved by many. Still, it falls short of being better or even equal to the original. It's decent, just not as good.

Third tasting, October 6, 2018: It was better having this again almost a year later with my more experienced nose and taste palate, and better overall whisky knowledge. Better than I remembered, and now highly recommended. I wouldn't say this whisky is complex, just busy, but in the right way. Lots to experience and find here, as it tastes more mature than the standard offering. Sharper smells than the original too. I recommend you add two spoons of water.

- **Nose:** Sharp, maple, fruity, caramel.
- **Palate:** Fruity (raisins, grapes, apples), vanilla. More potent than the standard Fuji-Sanroku.
- **Finish:** Powerful in the beginning (only if you didn't add water), turns to sweet vanilla soon after. Oily, dark fruits (same as the palate).
- **ABV:** 50%.
- **Distillery:** Fuji Gotemba.
- **Price:** ¥4,860 tax included (700ml).

#17

KIRIN PURE MALT WHISKY

In the subsequent Kirin reviews, you will hear me mention a lot about my visit to the Fuji Gotemba Distillery on November 7, 2017. I drank seven whiskies while there, and out of those, five were new first time tastings for me. This one, in particular, was the seventh and last whisky I had in that tasting session, but of course, the listings in this book are not in the order that I drank them in.

This whisky is a pure malt* (as the name states) that is a limited edition from Kirin. It is found only on-site at the Fuji Gotemba Distillery, and DRINX (the Japan-only, online Kirin shop).

Blender Motoki Takeshige, who isn't quite as famous or well-known as master blender Jota Tanaka, is responsible for this particular drink. This whisky, made from various kettles (initially used for grain whisky), and column stills, aims at creating a free-style blended malt whisky. It can be enjoyed comfortably either straight, on the rocks, with water, or in highballs, as stated by Takeshige. Kirin claims this has a light and soft, clean but rich taste.

*According to Japanese whisky terminology, a blend of many different malt whiskies.

- **Nose:** Pretty unpleasant strong malt aroma.
- **Palate:** Malty. Middle of the road in terms of strength, mild fruit taste, mild sweetness.
- **Finish:** Rounded. It leaves a lasting impression.
- **ABV:** 40%.
- **Distillery:** Fuji Gotemba.
- **Price:** ¥2,980 tax included (500ml).

#18

KIRIN WHISKEY PURE & MELLOW RIKU LAND DISCOVERY

Captain's Log, Stardate 2020.5.31. This is a current whisky review I'm sure no other book would have done. A week ago, I was able to stumble upon a new whisky release from Kirin. On May 20, 2020, Kirin released the Pure & Mellow as a replacement for their Fuji-Sanroku Tarujuku 50 Degrees that was discontinued last March 2019 due to a supply shortage.

The Pure & Mellow is roughly the same price as the Fuji-Sanroku. Hence, the question you probably are asking and want to be answered is, is it better?

The Pure & Mellow is a more profound maple nosing experience with grains, and the Fuji-Sanroku is a light maple with fumes (with no water added to each). The Fuji-Sanroku palate has a more vibrant, impactful flavor of malt & grains and a stronger cereal taste. I prefer the Fuji-Sanroku, but it all depends on if you want to go lighter or more intense. It's just way richer.

- **Nose:** Deep maple with grains.
- **Palate:** Oily & buttery, small vanilla, cream soda like after some time in the mouth. A little malty cereal, and minuscule spice.
- **Finish:** Quick terminating cream soda vanilla.
- **ABV:** 50%.
- **Distillery:** Fuji Gotemba.
- **Price:** ¥1,375 tax included (500ml).

#19

MARS BLENDED WHISKY SAIGO DON

This whisky is a limited edition made for 2018 commemorating the 150th anniversary of the Meiji Restoration. The Meiji Restoration was an event in 1868 Japan that restored practical imperial rule to the Empire of Japan by Emperor Meiji from the Tokugawa shogun dynasty and their administration.

According to whisky blogger Whiskey Richard, who I hold in acclaim from www.nomunication.jp, he says the Saigo Don from Mars Whisky was released on April 14, 2018. Unfortunately, production has ceased on this one, as it was limited to just a short run for this one year only. So should you find it, definitely don't leave it sitting on the shelf.

Captain's Log Supplemental 2020.5.6. I had at The Arty's Bar, Osaka, prior. Today I finally opened my own recently purchased personal bottle to do a taste reassessment. I couldn't ask for more with the price paid and the sophisticated, satisfying experience I got. Japanese whisky is so expensive these days it should be criminal. To think you can buy three of these for what one NAS Yamazaki cost, this makes for the better and more logical deal. And being a limited release too, it makes sense. One to drink, one to keep, and one to sell or trade. How can you go wrong?

- **Nose:** Very light, coconut, typical oak wood, and maple.
- **Palate:** Complex, creamy, and soft. Malty with light maple. Has a buttery texture.
- **Finish:** Quick finish that goes down smooth. Air-like peat-esque peat. It chews really lovely.
- **ABV:** 40%.
- **Distillery:** Tsunuki.
- **Price:** ¥2,750 tax included (700ml).

#20

MARS MALTAGE COSMO

Captain's Log, Stardate 2019.4.29. I was out on my second date with a current girlfriend at the time, and just as with the first date, we went out again to the fashionable and trendy neighborhood of Nakameguro, Tokyo. Just like me, a good time for her could be just sitting in a chill café for hours on end, relaxing, and enjoying the tranquility of the atmosphere. Charming décor and plush sofas or chairs are a must. Because it was deep into the evening, I took her to my "special place" which wasn't a café but the next best thing, a relaxed lounge bar called Cabin.

Frankly, when I go to bars now, I'm starting to have a hard time finding new experiences. I already had 93 distinctive entries of Japanese whiskies before this. It's not that I'm necessarily running out of whiskies, it's just getting tighter nevertheless to get new kicks.

Cosmo from the Mars Shinshu Distillery is a blended malt named after the 2,613.24 m Mt. Kosumo (越百山). It was initially released in 2015 at the Tokyo International Bar Show to much fanfare. Made from clean water rolling off the foot of the Kiso Mountains (also called the Central Alps) part of the Japanese Alps. The company says their whisky "expresses complexity and depth." While this whisky in no way knocked my socks off, I could enjoy it.

- **Nose:** Oak, vanilla, and toffee.
- **Palate:** Toffee, chocolate, buttery flavor (but not texture), oaky, and a little spicy.
- **Finish:** Smooth and long.
- **ABV:** 43%.
- **Distillery:** Shinshu.
- **Price:** ¥4,536 tax included (700ml).

#21

MARS THREE AND SEVEN 3 & 7

Captain's Log, Stardate 2020.6.8. OK, this is genuinely my final written review for this book. This whisky was matured in white oak barrels by Mars Whisky blender Hajime Kunai at the Mars Shinshu Distillery.

This is not a fact now, so definitely take it with a grain of salt. The Three And Seven is named so because apparently, it's a blend of 3-year-old grain whisky with 7-year-old malt whisky. If true, it shows the Japanese have really thought of some creative ways to label their whisky. That claim about the name or the ages of the blends is not mentioned anywhere on the distiller's website www.hombo.co.jp, but it appeared in the whisky's description on the Japanese auction website Rakuten and Amazon Japan where liquor can be sold.

You know, in Scotland, if you're going to put out an age statement blended whisky, you can only label it with the youngest aged whisky in the bottle, not the oldest. With the lax whisky laws in Japan, which really means none at all or lawless, you can kind of do as you want, just as long as you won't export it out of the country that is.

- **Nose:** Apricot.
- **Palate:** Watery light, oak, apricot, sweet cinnamon spice and chocolate.
- **Finish:** A quick one and done hit of maple sweetness.
- **ABV:** 40%.
- **Distillery:** Shinshu.
- **Price:** ¥1,540 tax included (720ml).

#22

MISAGO BLENDED WHISKY MATURED IN OAK BARREL

Misago is a cheap whisky that suddenly appeared for me one time back in 2017 at Aeon supermarket in Japan. There was one bottle on the shelf just looking at me all lonely, so I decided to buy it. I'll be damned. Some months later, the shelf at the same Aeon was full of it, along with a promo video of it playing on repeat. And then every subsequent Aeon I went to after that, I noticed this whisky there too. Now it just seems to be a staple of Aeon.

The appearances from Misago don't stop there; in 2019, for a little more than twice the price, the Sherry Cask Finish became available. Just last week around at the time of me writing this, on March 20, 2020, I saw a new Misago Bourbon Cask Finish Aged 5 Years Blended Whisky at Aeon.

Other than what's written on the bottle (of this and other Misago whiskies), the company behind it Minami (Southern) Alps Wine and Beverage Co. is quite incognito. There's a lot of mystique surrounding them and the whisky. You can't find much about it at all on the Internet, even in Japanese, and you'll be lucky if anything comes up at all if you Google it in English. All I can tell you is that they are from Fuefuki, Yamanashi Prefecture.

- **Nose:** Ethanol, oak wood, grapefruit.
- **Palate:** Sweet vanilla, creamy, malty.
- **Finish:** A strong bite that you can feel in your sinuses.
- **ABV:** 40%.
- **Distillery:** Minami Alps Wine and Beverage Co., Ltd.
- **Price:** ¥1,408 tax included (700ml).

#23

MISAGO BLENDED WHISKY BOURBON CASK FINISH AGED 5 YEARS

Captain's Log, Stardate 2020.6.7. Misago is an affordable whisky brand exclusive to and distributed by Aeon Liquor Co., Ltd. in Aeon supermarkets, but made by Minami Alps Wine and Beverage Co. It's probably not even Japanese, but that's speculative. The labeling doesn't say anywhere or allude to it as being "made in Japan," which is quite honest. And most of the Minami Alps products are imported in any case. As early as March this year, I began seeing this on shelves, making it the third Misago variant aside from the original I spotted.

This is malt and grain matured for 5 years in bourbon barrels. If those words 5年樽熟成 (5-year barrel aging) were not written on the bottle, you'd easily assume this was even younger than that based on how light the color of the whisky is. To the whisky novices, whisky extracts its color from the wood staves it comes into contact with while sitting inside the barrel. The longer it sits, the deeper and darker the color becomes. Whisky that we call "new make," a whisky that hasn't been placed into a barrel yet for maturation, will appear transparent in color. It looks very much like other clear spirits. So I mention this not because this seems like a new make whisky, but the visuals do give me a vibe of something that is only a few years old in terms of maturation.

- **Nose:** Vanilla and coconut.
- **Palate:** Creamy, light, and smooth vanilla.
- **Finish:** A unique finish with a quick burning bite, but relieving aftertaste.
- **ABV:** 40%.
- **Distillery:** Minami Alps Wine and Beverage Co., Ltd.
- **Price:** ¥1,815 tax included (700ml).

#24

NIKKA
BLACK NIKKA WHISKY
(FROM THE LATE 1980S)

Captain's Log, Stardate 2018.9.28. Another day another whisky at Bar UK, Osaka. The bar master Eiji-san gave me something special today, a unique blend of Black Nikka bottled in the late 80s. It gets rarer and rarer as time goes on. As if I needed to tell you. Trying to hunt this down on the Internet is difficult. I spotted one seller from Fukuoka, Japan, trying to sell an empty bottle on eBay for approximately ¥9,731 (USD 89.00). If I can find anything that resembles the bottle I drank from, the sellers really don't provide much information about what it is they have. I looked at many Japanese auction websites, and if I do find something of resemblance, no one offers a year or period it may be from. Your guess would be as good as mine as to what price to appraise these older bottles at.

It was June 1956 when the original Rare Old Black Nikka Whisky from the founding father of Japanese whisky, Masataka Taketsuru, debuted. Nine years after the first release, in 1965, Masataka made a renewed Black Nikka as a first grade blended whisky. It included malt and grains (the first whisky in Japan to include grains and distilled in an old fashion Coffey still). It combined strength and softness for a delicious tasting whisky. The bottle of this Black Nikka from the late 1980s closely resembles the one from 1965.

- **Nose:** Acetone cleaning solvent, afterward subsiding apples in the background.
- **Palate:** Ripe apples.
- **Finish:** Ripe apples.
- **ABV:** 42%.
- **Distillery:** Yoichi & Miyagikyo, Distilleries.
- **Price:** N/A (720ml).

#25

NIKKA
BLACK NIKKA SPECIAL

Captain's Log, Stardate 2017.12.8 21:36. I went to a branch of a bar chain called 82 Ale House near Kinshicho Station, a railway station in Sumida, (East) Tokyo, Japan. There they have many famous and popular whiskies from all over the world. There's a "tasting set" for ¥850 (which was once ¥1,080 at the time of review) and ¥680 during happy hour. If you don't want to order one single dram, you can get this discounted tasting set and choose three kinds of whisky from among over 40 brands. With the three whiskies you get, each glass will be a pour of 20ml. So I ordered this and got three Japanese whiskies (Black Nikka Special, Yoichi, and Taketsuru). For my tasting notes on each one, please refer to the respective page they are featured.

Black Nikka (nicknamed Black Beard) is a brand that debuted in 1956 and renewed in 1965 with the introduction of distilled grains into the mix. Since then, there have been many spin-off variations of it that have come out on the market. Such as the Black Nikka Clear Blend, Black Nikka Rich Blend, Black Nikka Deep Blend, anniversary bottlings, and annual limited editions. Nikka themselves describe this whisky as a harmony of malt and grain content.

- **Nose:** Sweet, some fruit, minimal alcohol.
- **Palate:** Heavy taste, intense oranges.
- **Finish:** The immediate aftertaste is nothing special, quite bland actually, but the long-term is quite pleasant.
- **ABV:** 42%.
- **Distillery:** Yoichi & Miyagikyo, Distilleries.
- **Price:** ¥1,340 tax included (720ml).

#26

NIKKA BLACK RICH BLEND

Captain's Log, Stardate 2019.11.16. Well, this is embarrassing. I first had this whisky in the summer of 2018, where I bought a small 180ml bottle for quite cheap from a Family Mart convenience store in Osaka. I guess I must've gone through the whole bottle without taking any tasting notes, which is the entire reason I bought it. To review. Luckily I had it again today at the Whisky Festival 2019 in Tokyo.

On the front of the bottle, Nikka wrote, "Rich and well-balanced taste for the casual whisky enthusiast." I'm not going to challenge that. For as cheap as I bought this 180ml bottle for sub 500 JPY, it was better than most competitively priced whiskies, although it isn't perfect.

This spin-off variation of the Black Nikka brand hit the market on March 26, 2013. It's a drink they highly recommend you use for drinking on the rocks. Nikka says this is a "whisky that is completely different from clear." I think that means their Nikka Black Clear brand, but I'm lost in translation on that one. "To achieve mellowness and a rich body, a gorgeous, fruity, and fragrant sherry barrel malt is used as the key malt." This is combined with distilled grains from a Coffey still to make a whisky that is full of richness.

- **Nose:** A chemical type of peat with sherry.
- **Palate:** Mellow, buttery, smooth taste.
- **Finish:** Initial light smoke, mellow linger.
- **ABV:** 40%.
- **Distillery:** Yoichi & Miyagikyo, Distilleries.
- **Price:** ¥1,166 tax included (700ml).

#27

NIKKA COFFEY GRAIN WHISKY

Captain's Log, Stardate 2018.9.14. On yet another routine journey to Bar UK, Osaka, I was able to give the Nikka Coffey Grain Whisky its time after much delay. Part of a pair of whiskies made in column "Coffey" stills (named after inventor Mr. Aeneas Coffey). The other being the Nikka Coffey Malt Whisky. This whisky is said to be made mostly with corn (and I suppose that means some barely).

While this has some bourbon elements in its making and smells a bit like bourbon, this is overall something different. It's better than many other Japanese grain whiskies I had (e.g., Suntory Chita, Kirin 2017 Distiller's Select Single Grain).

On Nikka's English website Nikka says, "The complex, sweet and mellow flavors of this expression will help you re-discover the beauty of a grain whisky." I must say I'd have to agree with them. I think it's a sweet whisky with some mild elements to it. I suppose you could call it complex. I recommend it to all takers; fans of Nikka whiskies and grain whiskies.

- **Nose:** A grainy bourbon-like smell. With vanilla and candy. It features a strong smell of marker or paints that I couldn't shake.
- **Palate:** Light fruits hit in the beginning, later comes watermelon.
- **Finish:** Watermelon and a hint of spice like smoke. Aftertaste of melon and vanilla.
- **Color:** Nice golden hue.
- **ABV:** 45%.
- **Distillery:** Miyagikyo.
- **Price:** ¥6,458 tax included (700ml).

#28

NIKKA COFFEY MALT WHISKY

Captain's Log. Stardate 2019.9.14. The place, Bar UK, Osaka, Japan. I'm enjoying this in the same tasting session as the Nikka Coffey Grain Whisky, the other part of this pair of whiskies made in column "Coffey" stills (named after inventor Mr. Aeneas Coffey). Both are good, but this is a better experience than the Coffey Grain. It certainly has a more pleasant nosing experience than the Coffey Grain, which smelt like markers.

This whisky is made from 100% malted barely but is categorized as a grain whisky by Nikka since it is not distilled in a pot still. It is made with a traditional continuous Coffey still that is more associated with corn grain whiskies. Nikka was trying to create a new flavor of whisky by using malted barley as a raw material in the still rather than a grain.

Websites The Whisky Exchange and Master of Malt both state this became apart of Nikka's permanent lineup in 2014. Unlike many other whiskies in Nikka's lineup, you're in luck if you're in the western market, as both this and the Coffey Grain are available in your region, that's not always the case. The other good thing about the USA bottlings is that you all get an extra 50ml of juice. Japan's standard bottling size for a majority of Japanese whiskies is 700ml.

- **Nose:** Super sweet vanilla, banana bread.
- **Palate:** Sweet with upfront chocolate, caramel, and fruits in the background.
- **Finish:** A continuation of that chocolate and caramel.
- **Color:** Gold.
- **ABV:** 45%.
- **Distillery:** Miyagikyo.
- **Price:** ¥6,458 tax included (700ml).

#29

NIKKA DATE

Captain's Log, Stardate 2018.10.13. Bar UK, Osaka, Japan. I've been on an extended mission this week, reviewing Nikka whiskies primarily, and here's an interesting one I found. A region exclusive. Named after Date Masamune, who ruled the Sendai area in feudal Japan in the early Edo period (1603-1868).

Nikka Date is a blended whisky sold only in Miyagi prefecture (and obviously online). A blend of malt and grain made in Coffey stills from 1963 Glasgow, which was once in the Nishinomiya plant, and later transferred to Miyagikyo. Masataka Taketsuru's goal with blended whiskies like this (and I guess all his whiskies) was to make Japanese whiskies comparable to those of Scotland. So Nikka says. Nikka describes this as having a "soft malty aroma, a sweet and smooth taste like vanilla, and a new flavor of blended whisky that combines strength and tenderness."

As mentioned, I first had this at Bar UK in 2018, and again a second time at the Whisky Festival 2019 in Tokyo on Saturday, November 16. I'm quite satisfied with it. My go-to phrase is that I've never been disappointed really by any Nikka whisky I tried before. This is not an exclusion of my convictions.

- **Nose:** Complex. Citric fruit and some solvent. Vanilla shows up after waiting some time.
- **Palate:** Sweet, solvent, light oil. Chocolate after letting sit in your mouth.
- **Finish:** Some smoke with chocolate.
- **ABV:** 43%.
- **Distillery:** Miyagikyo.
- **Price:** ¥4,000–¥5,000 online intra-Japan (700ml).

#30

NIKKA WHISKY TAKESTSURU PURE MALT

Captain's Log, Stardate 2017.12.8. At bar 82 Ale House, during my tasting session of three Nikkas, I had this. The Taketsuru Pure Malt is vatted malt from both of Nikka's distilleries, named after the company's founder Masataka Takesturu. I don't know if I would be wrong by calling Taketsuru Pure Malt the flagship line of the Nikka company, but I feel like this is the one. It represents the direction Nikka goes with their whiskies. Closer to Scotch with some liberties, rather than the Suntory route that is one headed in a new direction. Neither road is the right or wrong way, just different paths. This is a standout for the company, and bearing the founder's name on the bottle, it better be.

The Whisky Exchange website says, "Taketsuru's no-age-statement blended malt contains a high percentage of malt from Miyagikyo, with the remainder coming from Yoichi. Aged on average for around 10 years in a variety of different cask types, including some sherry wood for extra richness." Those words "on average for," they mess me about when hearing them used to refer to NAS whiskies. Be cautious when hearing them, because you'll never know what percentage of what age statement whiskies are used. The only absolutes are age statement whiskies with years written on the front of bottles.

- **Nose:** An initial spicy oak smell that quickly gives way to woody, sweet vanilla. Extremely pleasant.
- **Palate:** Spicy oak, smoky. Intense for its ABV.
- **Finish:** Vanilla. A smoky sensation is sent up into your sinuses with chewable wooded smoke.
- **Color:** Gold with pinkish hue.
- **ABV:** 43%.
- **Distillery:** Yoichi & Miyagikyo, Distilleries.
- **Price:** ¥4,818 tax included (700ml).

#31

NIKKA WHISKY TAKESTSURU AGED 12 YEARS PURE MALT

Captain's Log, Stardate 2018.10.12 19:10. Bar UK, Osaka. This is a vatting of 12 years old malts (and claimed older) from both of Nikka's distilleries. Unfortunately, as it goes, it has been discontinued due to the Japanese whisky boom and subsequent shortages. After much research on the Internet, the date of that discontinuation seems vague, but it seems to be circa 2014/2015.

This is a very Speyside-esque, sweet-smelling blend, and it is one of the, if not the smoothest, easiest to go down Nikkas I've tried. I've drunk so many now it's hard to say that definitively, but it's up there. When you just want to reach for something that you don't have to think about or assess, go for this one. It's a vatted malt that doesn't require much thought to get into. Just turn off your mind and relax.

"Taketsuru Pure Malt is a range of blended malt whiskies named in honor of Masataka Taketsuru, the founder of Nikka and father of Japanese whisky. These whiskies highlight the complexity and preciseness of blending." -Nikka

- **Nose:** Sweet, creamy, fruits. Vanilla on second nosing.
- **Palate:** Sweet, fruity (apples and oranges), caramel.
- **Finish:** Apples, buttery caramel. A light lingering of that same buttery caramel flavor.
- **Color:** Amber with a bronze highlight.
- **ABV:** 40%.
- **Distillery:** Yoichi & Miyagikyo, Distilleries.
- **Price:** Approximately ¥26,800 online intra-Japan (700ml).

NIKKA WHISKY TAKESTSURU AGED 17 YEARS PURE MALT

Captain's Log. Stardate 2018.10.12 19:50. Bar UK, Osaka. Nikka Taketsuru 17 is vatted malt from both of Nikka's distilleries, named after the company's founder Masataka Takesturu. The company's website calls him "the founder and father of Japanese whisky." When the former slave, Nearest Green, was Jack Daniel's master blender and teaching Jack the tricks of the distillation trade, it was Jack in the end who reaped the rewards. Why? Because Jack was the name on the bottle.

Similarly, it was Masataka Takestsuru, who joined Kotobukiya (now known as Suntory) in 1923 and was their original master blender. He taught the company's founder Shinjiro Torii what there is to know about whisky making. Suntory is the big name now around the world, but let's not forget who greatness in Japan started with.

I don't know if I would be wrong by calling Taketsuru Pure Malt the flagship line of the Nikka company, but I feel like this is the one. It represents the direction Nikka goes with their whiskies. Closer to Scotch with some liberties rather than the Suntory route, which is one headed in a new direction. Neither road is the right or wrong way, just different.

- **Nose:** Oaky, citrus, oranges. Vanilla on second nosing.
- **Palate:** Light smoke, woody, citrus.
- **Finish:** Complex, spicy, smoky, citrus.
- **Color:** Burnished gold with a copper hue.
- **ABV:** 43%.
- **Distillery:** Yoichi & Miyagikyo, Distilleries.
- **Price:** Approximately ¥23,000 online intra-Japan (700ml).

#33

NIKKA
THE NIKKA 12 YEARS OLD

Captain's Log, Stardate 2018.8.31. My Cameroonian friend Kenny, who resides in the Greater Tokyo Area, was the third person from that region to visit me in Osaka. This was when I held my five-month summer DJ residency at a downtown four-star hotel. After the gig, where he attended as a VIP, I introduced him to one of my new bar homes in Osaka (now in Tokyo) called The Arty's Bar. Arty's Bar was also downtown near Kita-Shinchi Station, where the hotel and Bar UK are. Kenny ordered a mojito, which is Arty's specialty, and I got a dram of this whisky.

To celebrate Nikka's 80th anniversary in 2014, Nikka introduced this blended whisky containing malt from Yoichi and Miyagikyo Distilleries, along with Coffey grain whisky. And as fast as this whisky showed up, is how quickly it left. In early 2019 it was announced this would be discontinued similarly to how a multitude of other aged Japanese whiskies was due to shortages of stock. And like all the other Japanese aged whiskies that left, it was replaced by a NAS whisky. The replacement called, The Nikka Tailored was introduced on April 9, 2019, and comes in the same bottling, but with different labeling. The emblem on both The Nikka 12 and Tailored was designed by Masataka Taketsuru in 1940. The bottle design was inspired by Kimonos.

- **Nose:** Sweet toffee, maple, and green apples.
- **Palate:** Buttery texture and light smoke.
- **Finish:** Light smoke with a medium spicy finish. Some of that green apple that appears on the nose shows up here.
- **ABV:** 43%.
- **Distillery:** Yoichi & Miyagikyo, Distilleries.
- **Price:** Approximately ¥10,000 online intra-Japan (700ml).

#34

NIKKA WHISKY
SINGLE MALT MIYAGIKYO

Captain's Log, Stardate 2018.8.3. About a little bit over half a year after having already tried the brother Yoichi (see that entry), I now move onto the Miyagikyo. This one I enjoyed at The Arty's Bar, Osaka. It comes from Nikka's second oldest distillery of the same name built in 1969 in the mountains of Sendai. With its mountainous and green forest area, mild climate, and soft water, the location of the Miyagikyo Distillery is in another dream location in Japan in the mind of its founder Masataka Taketsuru. A place where he could further realize his dreams of putting out the perfect Japanese whisky.

One thing about Nikka is that they are chock-full of blended whiskies. Finally, for a change, I'm reviewing a single malt. If I called the Taketsuru Pure Malt the flagship whisky of the entire company, this is more than likely the flagship or showcase whisky of Miyagikyo Distillery. In comparison to Yoichi, it's more substantial with its spices. And while the Yoichi has some sour apple notes, this features ripe red apples.

I added just a few drops of water to this one to help lighten it up a little. It was yet again another enjoyable offering. I think it's the 5th Nikka whisky I had, and I haven't been disappointed yet.

- **Nose:** Smooth sherry, light smoke, and heavy solvent-like odor.
- **Palate:** It's complex, textural, and crisp. Cinnamon spice, black licorice. A little bit of a tongue burn, it needs some drops of water.
- **Finish:** Quick delving deep smoke, turns smooth, subdued/soft licorice, red ripe apples.
- **Color:** Deep gold.
- **ABV:** 45%.
- **Distillery:** Miyagikyo.
- **Price:** ¥4,298 tax included (700ml).

#35

NIKKA WHISKY
SINGLE MALT YOICHI

Captain's Log, Stardate 2017.12.8. While at bar 82 Ale House, I indulged in a Nikka tasting session with this the Single Malt Yoichi, the Black Nikka Special, and Taketsuru Pure Malt. As previously mentioned, the tasting set sold at 82 Ale House lets patrons choose any three whiskies from among over 40 types of world whiskies. But of course, watching my diet, I had to stick to the program, so I had Japanese only on this night.

Yoichi is the flagship single malt from Nikka's first distillery of the same name. I was going to call this Nikka's rendition of Suntory's Hakushu as it has similar features. All things considered, since this came out first, let's say Hakushu is more like this. Founder Masataka Taketsuru chose Yoichi in Hokkaido because of its similarity to Scotland. In Japan, this would undoubtedly be the closest climate relative. In this whisky, you'll find elements of nature such as grass, peat, smoke, and fruits. Nikka says this was "crafted using methods from the past, such as direct coal heating." It is matured in ex-sherry casks.

- **Nose:** Scotch-like spice, but soft and easygoing. Vanilla.
- **Palate:** Peated smoke, mouthwatering citric oranges. A medium strength whisky without water dilution.
- **Finish:** Chewable, oily, grassy, and candied green apples. The aftertaste is the best part.
- **Color:** Vibrant gold.
- **ABV:** 45%.
- **Distillery:** Yoichi.
- **Price:** ¥4,298 tax included (700ml).

#36

NIKKA WHISKY
RARE OLD SUPER

Nikka Whisky Rare Old Super, also known as Super Nikka, is a blended malt and grain whisky released in October 1962 shortly after the death of Masataka Taketsuru's wife Rita a year before. This whisky is a dedication to her.

In March 2015, a limited reprint of the first issued Super Nikka with the original 1962 label was released. Whether it tastes different from what I'm reviewing now, I can't confirm as I haven't had it, but be aware that it exists. There are four versions of Super Nikka out now, a 700ml, 500ml, 50ml miniature, and a 300ml 12% abv canned highball.

Captain's Log, Stardate 2018.6.8. I'm at the sports bar Balabushka in Shinsaibashi, Osaka, where I got this cheap. Getting into it, this was one of the worst whiskies I had. Some that come to mind that could be worse are the Suntory yellow label, white label Kakubin whiskies, and the Top Value Whisky found at Aeon supermarkets.

Captain's Log Supplemental 2020.4.6. In Osaka, maybe it was the tumbler glass I got served in why I didn't like it, who knows. However, a second trial reveals it is better than memory serves, although still not the best Nikka whisky.

- **Nose:** Has a bland, generic smell—light oak.
- **Palate:** Mild strength, sherry spice, and chocolate.
- **Finish:** Buttery smooth, chocolate. The passage of time will reveal a mellow lingering of vanilla.
- **Color:** Burnished gold with orange hue.
- **ABV:** 43%.
- **Distillery:** Yoichi & Miyagikyo, Distilleries.
- **Price:** ¥2,610 tax included (700ml).

#37

SUNTORY THE CHITA

This is a Japanese single grain whisky that debuted in 2014 from the Suntory distillery of the same name (Chita Distillery). Chita is Suntory's third distillery located in the Port of Nagoya of Chita city. The distillery predominantly produces three types of grain whisky—light, medium, and heavy by a continuous distillation process using two to four columns. They then age in different casks and are combined to make the whisky.

This is not exactly flying off the shelf type whisky anywhere in Japan. Go into any given supermarket or liquor store in Japan, and you'll find an abundance of this just lingering on the shelf. To its credit, it is showing up in more Japanese izakayas (a type of Japanese dining bar that serves an assortment of inexpensive dishes and bar food). So far, the NAS version is the only one available; one can only assume in the future aged versions will eventually come out. Some special editions have come out, though, for example, The Essence of Suntory Chita Distillery Wine Cask Finish.

Captain's Log Supplemental. Stardate 2018.9.14. I retried my bottle of Chita sometime after my initial tasting. With an increase in my tasting experiences, where I disliked something before, it has now grown on me. I've come to appreciate it.

- **Nose:** Grainy with a light washboard marker smell to it.
- **Palate:** Buttery, oranges, light spice, artificial smoke.
- **Finish:** Rich and sweet, vanilla, oranges.
- **Color:** Bright gold.
- **ABV:** 43%.
- **Distillery:** Chita.
- **Price:** ¥4,082 tax included (700ml)

#38

SUNTORY THE HAKUSHU SINGLE MALT WHISKY DISTILLER'S RESERVE

This was the first-ever, official whisky review that I've conducted for my YouTube channel The Gentleman's Club. The date was August 13, 2017. Watching those early videos makes me cringe because I can see I was new and trying to find my voice and how to express myself eloquently. Boy, was it painful to watch. No matter what I or anyone else thinks of the video, I still stand by my word on what I said about the whisky. By the way, that video may already be deleted by now and replaced with an updated review. Just in case you decide to go looking for it.

From the mountain forest distillery of the same name that opened in 1973, The Hakushu is a single malt that focuses on nature. From the clean waters flowing down from the beautiful Southern Japanese Alps to the forest, it truly is a reflection of the environment from which it comes. With its green, grassy, and fruity notes. This whisky was the vision of Suntory's second master blender Keizo Saji, whose goal was to create an all-new whisky experience.

I delved into this whisky from Japan's biggest distributor of whiskies and was pleasantly surprised. I found that at 43% abv, it was quite intense. Usually, 43% is light when it comes to whisky. I had a burning sensation going on for the finish.

- **Nose:** Floral, everything green (green apple, pear, grass).
- **Palate:** A slight spice with green fruits (green apples and pears). Buttery.
- **Finish:** Subtle smoke.
- **Color:** Light gold.
- **ABV:** 43%.
- **Distillery:** Hakushu.
- **Price:** ¥4,536 tax included (700ml).

#39

SUNTORY HIBIKI JAPANESE HARMONY

Hibiki (響) means sound, reverberation, echo, and resonance in Japanese. As Suntory tells it, Hibiki, the whisky resonates from "Japanese nature and its artistic sensibilities." Time, as it is associated with Hibiki, is represented by the glass bottle with its twenty-four facets, which features a handcrafted washi (traditional Japanese paper) label.

In 1987 research began to make this blended whisky from both malt and grain, and it was finally birthed in 1989 to celebrate 90 years of Suntory whisky. Today it is comprised of thirty malt and grain whiskies from all three of Suntory's distilleries to make this harmonious blend of excellence.

Hibiki was the first famous Suntory whisky I tried in my life, and one of the first I learned to love at the time I first started consuming whisky. I learned about it just as how many others did, by watching the movie *Lost in Translation* back in 2003. I recall trying it first at bars on about two occasions before I was able to finally acquire my first bottle of it at a local supermarket in Japan.

Compared to the vintage version, it's similar. While it's more robust, it's still very light. I prefer the old version.

- **Nose:** Floral notes, woodiness.
- **Palate:** Honey, candied oranges.
- **Finish:** Mizunara with light spice.
- **Color:** Amber.
- **ABV:** 43%.
- **Distillery:** Yamazaki, Hakushu, and Chita, Distilleries.
- **Price:** ¥5,378 tax included (700ml).

SUNTORY HIBIKI BLENDER'S CHOICE

Captain's Log, Stardate 2018.9.11. Bar UK, Osaka. At the time of me writing this very entry, just a week ago today is when this new Hibiki offering called the Blender's Choice was released. It is to replace the now discontinued Hibiki 17 Years Old on the retail market. I was looking forward to trying this with much anticipation. I finally got my wish to do so on the same night I got to try both the Suntory Whisky Hibiki (Vintage) and Hibiki 12 Years Old whiskies for the first time.

Suntory says this blended whisky comes from various carefully selected barrels ranging in age from around 15 years' average, and some more than 30 years. Something about this sounds so fishy to me. You can think what you want, but I don't believe these numbers at all. If Suntory had to discontinue the Hibiki 17 due to shortage of stock but can put out a multitude of age 15 year oldish Hibiki... How? Why?

Blender's Choice is just slightly more intense than the Japanese Harmony I'd say by one notch. It's more mature tasting, yes, but I don't see that big of a difference between the two myself to warrant this having been produced.

- **Nose:** Ethanol. It doesn't smell like much of anything. You have to reach deep to find that wine cask aroma.
- **Palate:** Oranges, and wine. Heavier than the Hibiki Japanese Harmony NAS.
- **Finish:** Red wine (woody).
- **ABV:** 43%.
- **Distillery:** Yamazaki, Hakushu, and Chita, Distilleries.
- **Price:** ¥11,800 tax included (700ml).

#41

SUNTORY KAKUBIN

Suntory Kakubin (square bottle), aka Suntory Whisky, is one of Suntory's oldest brands, and possibly it's current, most basic offering you can get. It's been around since 1937 and is available throughout Japan obviously, and Southeast Asia. A mix from barrels that come from both the Yamazaki and Hakushu Distillery. Suntory says it "features a sweet aroma, a thick body, and a dry afterglow." I think that's so full of it.

They recommended you use this for making a highball. To that I say, any whisky that can't stand on its own merit, stand-alone, not mixed with anything, isn't good at all. That doesn't stop many Japanese from liking this, and they do drink it the recommended way. Jack Daniels is a whisky used in cocktails in America, and it's good enough to have stand-alone and is still affordable.

This really needs the quality upped to make it a better value drink. There are so many Japanese whiskies on the market for cheaper that are better, for example, from Akashi. I don't know why one would reach for this. It looks high quality sitting in its tortoise-shell designed bottle, with gold font, and Suntory's coat of arms in gold foil, you'd think you were about to drink something made for a king. However, that's not the case.

- **Nose:** Ethanol and honey.
- **Palate:** Quick and potent.
- **Finish:** Taste like how isopropyl alcohol smells.
- **ABV:** 40%.
- **Distillery:** Yamazaki and Hakushu, Distilleries.
- **Price:** ¥1,382 tax included (700ml).

#42

SUNTORY WHISKY ROYAL BLENDED WHISKY

Captain's Log, Stardate 2019.3.16. In the heart of Tokyo, at a Metro subway station called Hiro-o, there's a high-class hotel operated by the US Navy open to all servicemen and their dependents called The New Sanno. I had been here before as a patron and as a DJ. On this date, I attended a St. Patrick's Day DJ event inside of the Fair Winds American cocktail lounge. There I spotted something new (new drink for me, but it's been around for almost 60 years) on the menu I never had before, the Suntory Whisky Royal. The asking price was $8.00 US a shot, not knowing whether it was worth that price or not, I chanced it, and I was pleasantly surprised.

If you're being pessimistic, you'd say this is a safe bet for a dram, passable, adequate. If you're having a good day and are optimistic, you might say a little better than an average affair. I'm leaning to the optimistic side.

This malt and grain whisky is the final work of Shinjiro Torii and was introduced in 1960 to celebrate Suntory's 60th anniversary as a beverage making company (not as a whisky maker). By the time this book releases in 2020, it'll be the 60th anniversary of this whisky. Interesting fact: the cork stopper is shaped like a mini torii gate.

- **Nose:** Creamy vanilla.
- **Palate:** Smooth, buttery, toffee. A taste of chocolate develops after letting sit on the tongue.
- **Finish:** Palate flavors subside almost immediately.
- **ABV:** 43%.
- **Distillery:** Yamazaki (assumed).
- **Price:** ¥3,218 tax included (700ml).

#43

SUNTORY WHISKY TORYS CLASSIC

Captain's Log, Stardate 2017.8.24. Home. Torys Classic is one of the oldest offerings from Suntory, having been around since 1946 shortly after the war. If you can see the progression in the bottles and labelings, it has gone through at least eight variations before the design you see now. The current design has a black label with a gold tumbler shaped glass in the center, and TORYS wrote very big and bold in the middle of that glass. You can buy it in many different sizes, as it comes in 180ml / 700ml / 1800ml / 2700ml / 4000ml sizes; however, I just purchased a standard 700ml bottle from the supermarket. I think this is Suntory's cheapest whisky.

I'm assuming this comes from the Yamazaki Distillery since it predates both of the other Suntory distilleries by a little than over 25 years. Because this doesn't meet quality standards in the EU, it can't be labeled and sold as whisky. It would be illegal. This comes from the fact that anything under 40% abv isn't considered whisky. This only has an abv of 37%. Japan itself is very lax to virtually all regulations.

Suntory says, "It features a gentle, sweet fragrance and a rounded, smooth taste. The well-balanced taste can be enjoyed not only as a highball but also on the rocks or with water."

- **Nose:** Ethanol, honey.
- **Palate:** Very light, almost like water.
- **Finish:** Mild punch.
- **ABV:** 37%.
- **Distillery:** Yamazaki (assumed).
- **Price:** ¥753 tax included (700ml).

SUNTORY TORYS EXTRA HONEY

Captain's Log, Stardate 2017.8.24. Home. Released on September 18, 2012, Torys Extra Honey is a spinoff of the previous entry Torys Classic. And like that entry, it would be illegal to classify it as whisky just about anywhere in the world. It sits at 20% abv, well below the 40% abv minimum required by law. However, Torys Extra Honey doesn't claim to be a whisky. It's ready to serve whisky liqueur, an alcoholic drink composed of distilled spirits, and additional flavorings. It's very sweet, so clearly it is full of sugar. It also has lemon spirits, honey, acidulant, and spice. Torys Extra Honey is most comparable to the Jack Daniels and Jim Beam honey renditions of their leading drinks.

Also, let me not forget to mention, this is only available for a limited time only. As I'm updating this entry on January 7, 2020, I don't see this anymore in supermarkets. Whereas, around the time I bought it, it was abundant in them.

Judging it for what it is, a whisky liqueur, it's quite a delicious drink. Better than the Classic, I'm ashamed to say. If you don't like extra sweet, this definitely won't be for you.

- **Nose:** Pleasant, sweet like candy.
- **Palate:** Flavorful honey.
- **Finish:** N/A.
- **ABV:** 20%.
- **Distillery:** N/A.
- **Price:** ¥490 tax included (300ml).

#45

SUNTORY WORLD WHISKY AO

The press release for this new premium blended whisky came out on January 10, 2019, with the actual product release happening on April 16, 2019. Sold exclusively in Japan with limited availability, Suntory's fifth-generation chief blender, Shinji Fukuyo, brings us the company's first-ever globally blended whisky.

The whisky is sourced from seven Suntory Group-owned distilleries spanning five of the world's most famous whisky-regions; Japan, the United States, Scotland, Canada, and Ireland. The whisky contains liquid produced "through several fermentation techniques, shapes and sizes of pot stills, and by using an assortment of casks."

Some interesting tidbits about this whisky, the word Ao (碧) in Japanese, means bright blue in color. As weird as this may sound, apparently, it means green too. If you type the kanji into Google Images, you'll get varying results. Still, you'll mostly see a greenish-blue/cyan type color. The shape of the bottle from an overhead view is that of a diamond with five corners, each representing one of the significant whisky regions of the world.

Tastewise it is very comparable to that of the Suntory Hibiki Japanese Harmony.

- **Nose:** It's dominately fruity, minuscule creamy, and has a little bit of cinnamon spice.
- **Palate:** Accessible & simple, light. Buttery & oily. Green apples.
- **Finish:** Smooth finish, and like the palate buttery/oily.
- **ABV:** 43%.
- **Distillery:** The Yamazaki (Japan), Hakushu (Japan), Admore (Scotland), Glen Garioch (Scotland), Jim Beam (USA), Alberta (Canada), and Couley (Ireland) Distilleries.
- **Price:** ¥5,500 tax included (700ml).

#46

SUNTORY YAMAZAKI DISTILLERY SINGLE MALT WHISKY (DISTILLERY ONLY)

In Osaka, parallel to and across from the Dojima River, there is the Suntory Holdings Limited Osaka Head Office building. That's a mouthful to say. Inside this building on the first floor, there used to be a specialty shop called the Suntory Whisky Shop W. You could buy liquor inside, and there may have even been a bar. A series of exclusive 300ml bottles of Yamazaki and Hakushu was sold here under the name Whisky Shop W. Unfortunately, in March 2016, this shop closed. Meaning they would cease with these exclusive releases too.

The Suntory Yamazaki Distillery Single Malt Whisky from the Yamazaki Distillery is the spiritual successor to the Suntory Whisky Shop W. WSO-009. Let me tell you it's not the same whisky. The only similarities are in the bottle shape, box, and name. It's actually the same bottling and box, but the labeling and artwork are different. It's a lighter abv, and the fruits this time around are apples instead of strawberries. It's lacking the candied sweet smell and the peat-like taste and finish of the WSO-009.

I'd say it's worth a buy as a souvenir or collectors' whisky for its price point and limited availability. I've had better apple whiskies before that taste riper, or more like apple skin, but this is adequate.

- **Nose:** Spicy, apples.
- **Palate:** Apples and apple juice.
- **Finish:** Short, mild spice, apples in the back.
- **ABV:** 40%.
- **Distillery:** Yamazaki.
- **Price:** ¥1,500 (300ml).

SUNTORY THE YAMAZAKI SINGLE MALT WHISKY DISTILLER'S RESERVE

This is an excellent whisky just to be a NAS. The Yamazaki Distiller's Reserve is one of the first purchases I made in my whisky endeavors. I was really, genuinely impressed with it. It has a Japanese identity all on its own very far removed from what you would expect from Scotch whiskies. That's the whole point and the thing that Suntory was going for. They were always trying to make an original identity for Japanese whisky.

Let's try not to get confused here. The Yamazaki Distillery was built in 1923 (as shown on the bottle). It started distilling in 1924, and the first whisky was released in 1929, which wasn't this. It's actually called Suntory Whisky, aka Shirofuda (White Label). Suntory's second master blender Keizō Saji (November 1, 1919–November 3, 1999), son of founder Shinjiro Torii, released the Suntory Single Malt Whisky Yamazaki in 1984. There's kind of a play on years shown on the bottle to make you believe the history behind this single malt is older than it really is.

Back to the whisky in hand. Let me state for the record, I do prefer this one more than The Yamazaki Aged 12 Years. This was a reasonably priced whisky before around ¥4,500, but even the demand here led to increased prices of NAS in most places.

- **Nose:** Mostly berries (cherries and strawberries), with a little bit of chocolate, and mizunara oak.
- **Palate:** Milk chocolate, and raspberry.
- **Finish:** Creamy and smooth, some vanilla, and a long-lasting, chewable and lingering raspberry flavor.
- **Color:** Gold.
- **ABV:** 43%.
- **Distillery:** Yamazaki.
- **Price:** ¥8,800 before tax (700ml).

#48

SUNTORY THE YAMAZAKI SINGLE MALT WHISKY AGED 12 YEARS

I stumbled upon the Yamazaki 12 by accident the very first time I bought it in September 2017. At the time, I use to frequent a supermarket called Aeon to buy groceries. Inside this supermarket, there's an international section full of alcoholic beverages from all over the world, and they have an excellent whisky section. About once every three months, you might come upon a rare whisky, and if you don't take the opportunity to buy it on the spot, it will disappear that day. You'll be waiting for months to try to obtain it again. My advice to you all is to seize opportunities. At the time, I was lucky to buy my bottle for just ¥9,000.

With the excitement I had for this, you'll be shocked to hear I'm just not a fan of the Yamazaki 12. I feel it falls short of being an excellent ambassador to the rest of the line compared to its younger and older brothers. If you like it, I'm really happy for you. For me, there is something about the fake smoke I don't like. It tastes a bit artificial. If you take my word for it, try before you buy.

I've been drinking this quite a bit over the past two years, and I think it's an adequate whisky. It is getting better and more tolerable with time, but as I said, it's just not as good as the NAS or other age statement variations.

- **Nose:** Peat esque smoke, vanilla, mizunara, oranges, and sweet candied fruits, among other fruits.
- **Palate:** Peat esque smoke and spice, oranges with other fruits.
- **Finish:** Long finish with light smoke, butter, and cinnamon.
- **Color:** Pure gold.
- **ABV:** 43%.
- **Distillery:** Yamazaki.
- **Price:** ¥23,544 tax included (700ml).

#49

SUNTORY THE YAMAZAKI SINGLE MALT WHISKY AGED 18 YEARS

Once upon a time in 2017, this was my favorite Japanese malt whisky, that is until 2018 came along. Though that's a story for another time. As Suntory's flagship single malt (and for the price you pay to play), you really do expect this whisky to deliver, and it does. It's complicated enough with subtle changes happening throughout your drinking experience from nosing to finish to give you an adventure. Still, it's not overly complicated to the point the nuances and beauty of it get lost on you along the way.

Suntory claims The Yamazaki is the No.1 single malt in Japan. I believe it is plausible while I don't have the sales data to confirm or refute that claim. As personally bearing witness to its popularity in whisky forums and groups, and scarcity on shelves. The aged 18 years is the sweet spot in the lineup for price and taste, arguably making it the most popular.

I was lucky enough to secure my purchase of this retail in Aeon supermarket on Christmas day for ¥30,000. Unfortunately, collectors (those people I despise that buy and never drink) helped contribute to soaring prices of this and other Japanese whiskies worldwide, including intra-Japan. Now, exactly a year after I bought it, it can be found for ¥70,000 on the whisky market.

- **Nose:** Spicy mizunara, raisins, vanilla.
- **Palate:** Spicy mizunara, dark chocolate, raisins.
- **Finish:** A smooth, quick delving spice. Lingering fruits (berries), and vanilla.
- **Color:** Deep amber.
- **ABV:** 43%.
- **Distillery:** Yamazaki.
- **Price:** ¥70,000 online (700ml).

#50

THE *Distilleries*

CHICHIBU DISTILLERY (SAITAMA)

Founder Ichiro Akuto established Venture Whisky Ltd. in 2004 and built Chichibu, his independent distillery in 2007. In the city of the same name, it is located about some 100 km (62 mi) northwest of Tokyo Station (depending on how you travel there) in the westernmost part of Saitama Prefecture.

Chichibu Distillery is most famously known for its brand line of whisky called "Ichiro's" that is named after its owner. Unbeknownst to some, Ichiro's family has been running a sake and shochu business since 1625, almost some 400 years. His grandfather Isouji Akuto built the Hanyu Distillery in 1941 and obtained a distiller's license after World War II. His father, Yutaka Akuto, later managed that distillery. Unfortunately, Hanyu was closed down in the year 2000 because of a recession in the economy.

The new owners of that distillery were not interested in distilling whisky because they thought it was a market soon coming to an end. With that knowledge, Ichiro was able to obtain the unwanted stills and casks from there, and use them as a basis to start a new whisky venture in 2008.

Today, the offerings from the distillery are rare and hard to come by. Ichiro has said he does not want his whisky sold in supermarkets or convenience stores. Instead, you must buy them online or from specialty liquor stores.

- **Address:** 〒368-0067 埼玉県秩父市みどりが丘 49
Midorigaoka 49, Chichibu, Saitama 〒368-0067
- **Access:** About 2 hours 20 minutes by train from Tokyo Station. 21 minutes by taxi from Seibu-Chichibu Station.
12 minutes by taxi from Minano Station.
- **Tel:** 0494-62-4601
- **Open Hours:** 9:00–17:00. Closed on some national holidays, and New Year.
- **Website:** https://www.facebook.com/ChichibuDistillery/

CHITA DISTILLERY (AICHI)

Suntory Chita Distillery Co., Ltd. is a grain whisky distillery jointly established by the Suntory Group with the Zennō Group. Founded in 1972 by Keizo Saji, the second master blender and son of company founder Shinjiro Torii, the Chita Distillery was the second built Suntory distillery after Yamazaki. It's located on the shores of the Chita Peninsula in Aichi Prefecture just south of Nagoya City. The distillery was purpose-built by Keizo to create the highest-quality Japanese grain whisky.

Using a continuous multiple column distillation process, Suntory has been distilling grain whisky from corn as the main ingredient since 1973. The distillery makes three types of grain whiskies: a Heavy-type grain whisky distilled through two columns, a medium-type through three columns, and a clean-type through four columns. The grain is featured in their highly rated Hibiki blended whisky and their affordable Kakubin whisky. It is also mixed with other whiskies from the Yamazaki and Hakushu Distilleries.

In September 2015, The Chita Suntory Whisky debuted, Suntory's first single grain whisky. It was made by Suntory's fifth-generation chief blender Fukuyo Shinji who selected ten-grain types to make the blend. Currently, it is sold in 700ml and 180ml sizes and has been discontinued in the 350ml size. The Essence of Suntory Whisky: Chita Distillery Wine Cask 4 Year Finish, Distilled in 2001 Bottled in 2018, is a 500ml limited edition release.

- **Address:** 〒478-0046 愛知県知多市北浜町16番地
16 Kitahamamachi, Chita, Aichi 〒478-0046
- **Tel:** 0562-32-6351
- **Open Hours:** The Chita Distillery is not open to the public.
- **Website:** https://whisky.suntory.com/en/global/distilleries/chita

EIGASHIMA DISTILLERY (HYOGO)

Formerly the White Oak Whisky Distillery, the distillery was renamed to the Eigashima Distillery in 2019. Eigashima Shuzo Co. Ltd. acquired their whisky manufacturing license in year 8 (1919) of the Taishō period (aka Taishō era) and are the first to obtain a license to make whisky according to their website. To explain what is the Taishō period, it is a period in Japanese history spanning from July 30, 1912, to December 25, 1926 coinciding with the rule of the Emperor, Yoshihito who was simply called Emperor during his life rule of Japan and posthumously known as Emperor Taishō.

All this information about 1919 is very vague because it isn't stated by Eigashima whether or not they began producing whisky in that year, or just obtained a license but hasn't started producing whisky yet. It is common knowledge that Suntory with their Yamazaki Distillery was the first to begin commercially producing whisky in 1924. The current White Oak Whisky Distillery was completed in year 59 (1984) of the Showa period. So what has Eigashima been doing between the years 1919 to 1984? Have they just been producing sake and shochu only or have they made any whisky in that time as well? If they have then I can't find any evidence of any whisky they made before 1984. I just have so many unanswered questions.

■ **Address:** 〒674-0065 兵庫県明石市大久保町西島919番地3
919-3 Nishijima, Okubo-cho, Akashi-shi, Hyōgo 〒674-0065
■ **Access:** About 57 minutes by train from Osaka Station. 8 minutes from Nishi-Eigashima Station.
■ **Tel:** 078-946-1001
■ **Open Hours:** Mon–Fri 9:00–17:00. Closed Sat, Sun, on some national holidays, and New Year.
■ **Website:** http://www.ei-sake.jp/

FUJI GOTEMBA DISTILLERY (SHIZUOKA)

The Kirin story. A lot of people outside of Japan to their knowledge may believe Kirin just to be only a whisky distillery, or a brewery, or both. Actually though for the unknowing, it is, in fact, a beverage company in general. Established as Japan Brewery Co., Ltd. in 1885 (the forerunner of Kirin Brewery Co., Ltd.), they make the prior mentioned drinks as well as other wine and liquors, soft drinks, teas, and green teas, juices, and more. Competitor Suntory like its rival Kirin is also a major Japanese beverage company not only known for whisky in Japan.

Kirin Holdings Company, Limited became incorporated on February 23, 1907, with their only whisky distillery being founded in 1972. Fuji Gotemba Distillery is located at the foot of Mt. Fuji in the city of Gotemba, Shizuoka prefecture 620 m (2034 ft) above sea level, with an average annual temperature of 13°C (55°F). From Tokyo station, it is located southwest about two hours thirty-minutes away by local train rides on the Tokaido and Gotemba train lines.

I first visited here on Tuesday, November 14, 2017. Hardly a date to tour a distillery. Luckily for me, there were not so many people, so I was able to go on a guided tour without a prior scheduled appointment. It is recommended though you schedule an appointment for here and all other distilleries in Japan to avoid disappointment after long journeys. I thought the facility was rather large and clean. The bar and shop were relaxing and organized.

■ **Address:** 〒412-0003 静岡県御殿場市柴怒田 970
970 Shibanta, Gotembashi, Shizuoka-ken 〒412-0003
■ **Access:** Free shuttle bus service from JR Gotemba Station Otome Exit. Board at the station roundabout. 20 minutes by taxi.
■ **Tel:** 0550-89-4909
■ **Open Hours:** 9:00–17:00. Closed every Monday (however, it will be open if Monday is a public holiday), year-end/New Year's holidays, equipment inspection days, etc.
■ **Website:** www.kirin.co.jp/entertainment/factory/english/whisky/
https://www.kirin.co.jp/products/whisky_brandy/gotemba/

HAKUSHU DISTILLERY (YAMANASHI)

Founded in 1973 by Keizo Saji, the son of company founder Shinjiro Torii. The Hakushu Distillery was Suntory's third built distillery but is sometimes considered the second because it is the second wholly-owned one. Saji's aim was to find a location with pristine water. He declared this location in a forest by Mt. Kaikomagatake in the Southern Alps mountain range to be it.

The environment and climate changes of the area are different enough to that of the Suntory Yamazaki Distillery to give whiskies made here a separate and distinctive flavor of their own. The Hakushu Single Malt Whisky that is made here and named after the distillery, is a drink that reflects its environment and evokes thoughts of greenery and nature. Inside the Hakushu compound, there are some similarities to the Yamazaki Distillery. It features six wash stills, six spirit stills, a bar, gift shop, and museum. What's different is that it has an indoor/outdoor restaurant called The Terrace and a "Bird Sanctuary" conservation on the premises.

The Hakushu Distillery is a more unique and exclusive experience than Yamazaki. Almost all Japanese whisky loving Japanophiles who come to Japan go to Osaka, Kyoto, and the Yamazaki Distillery because of its easy accessibility. To get to the Hakushu Distillery, it is more of a trip that involves a lot more travel and time, and trickier for tourists who don't have a grasp of the language. So naturally, it's just going to have fewer foreign visitors.

■ **Address:** 〒408-0316 山梨県北杜市白州町鳥原2913-1
2913-1 Torihara, Hakushu-cho, Hokuto-shi, Yamanashi Prefecture 〒408-0316
■ **Access:** About 2 hours by train from Shinjuku Station. Take the JR Limited Express "Azusa" train to Kobuchizawa Station.
■ **Tel:** 0551-35-2211
■ **Open Hours:** 9:30—16:30 (Last entry at 16:00). Closed over the New Year's holiday and during distillery shutdowns (some of which are not scheduled in advance).
■ **Website:** https://www.suntory.com/factory/hakushu/

MIYAGIKYO DISTILLERY (MIYAGI)

West of Sendai, and near the border of Yamagata Prefecture, is the home of Nikka's second distillery, Miyagikyo. Opened in 1969, this was an area founder Masataka Taketsuru set his sights on to expand and diversify his company's whiskies. Located in a forest with a cool climate, surrounded by mountains and two clean rivers (the Hirose River and the Shinkawa River). This was another excellent and quintessential location to set up shop. Taketsuru always wanted to match and make the Japanese equivalent to Scotch. So here, he produced grain whisky for blending to achieve the taste he wanted.

Today there are two running sets of Coffey stills in Miyagikyo. They "were first installed at the Nishinomiya plant and later transferred to Miyagikyo Distillery in 1999." Nikka states, "Coffey Stills, which are no longer rare in the world, has a lower degree of alcohol refining and distillation efficiency than other continuous stills. But it still has the right sweetness and flavor components in the distilled liquid. That is the taste of grain whisky that Masataka has sought. Tasty Coffey grain whisky is indispensable to Nikka's blended whiskey."

Many of Nikka's blended whiskies are partly produced at Miyagikyo, along with at Yoichi. Some whisky, such as the Date, Miyagikyo, Nikka Coffey Grain, and Nikka Coffey Malt, are solely made at Miyagikyo. By having a different distillation method at Miyagikyo, along with different shaped pot stills, Taketsuru worked towards creating an absolute contrast between the two distilleries.

■ **Address:** 〒989-3433 宮城県仙台市青葉区ニッカ1−番地 Miyagi, Sendai, Aoba Ward, Nikka 1 〒989-3433
■ **Access:** About 110 minutes by shinkansen from Tokyo Station to Sendai Station. By train 40 minutes from Sendai Station to Sakunami Station. Walking 25 minutes from Sakunami Station.
■ **Tel:** 22-395-2865
■ **Open Hours:** 9:00–16:30. Closed over the New Year's holiday and during distillery shutdowns. Some of which are not scheduled in advance.
■ **Website:** https://www.nikka.com/eng/distilleries/miyagikyo/

YAMAZAKI DISTILLERY (OSAKA)

Founded in 1923 by Shinjiro Torii, the Yamazaki Distillery is Japan's first and oldest malt distillery. Located on the Osaka/Kyoto border, around this area is where the Katsura, Uji, and Kizu rivers converge. Three rivers whose source is Lake Biwa in Shiga Prefecture just north. Lake Biwa is the largest freshwater lake in Japan, and good water is absolutely essential to making good whisky. Water is used in everything from malting, to mashing and diluting. So you can see why having one of Japan's softest waters as a source is integral to making great whisky. Part two of making great whisky is climate. "The diversity of this region's temperature and humidity creates ideal conditions for cask aging."

"Inspired by traditional Scottish whisky, Torii envisioned a Japanese approach by choosing a terrain and climate completely different from those of Scotland to create a unique kind of whisky." Torii's vision was to create an original Japanese whisky with a distinctive Japanese taste of its own. In contrast, his master blender Masataka Taketsuru wanted to create whisky closer to Scotch. But that's a story for another time.

The flagship Yamazaki Single Malt Whisky that began being made here in 1984 by the second master blender Keizo Saiji, son of Shinjiro Torii, is named after the distillery. For making whisky, the distillery features six wash stills and six spirit stills. For visitors, there's a bar, gift shop, and museum. Tours are also available.

■ **Address:** 〒618-0001大阪府三島郡島本町山5-2-1
5-2-1 Yamazaki, Shimamoto-cho, Mishima-gun, Osaka 〒618-0001
■ **Access:** 15 minutes by train from Kyoto Station or 26 minutes from Osaka Station to Yamazaki Station on JR Tokaido Line. 30 minutes by train from Umeda Station to Oyamazaki Station on Hankyu Kyoto Line.
■ **Tel:** 075-962-1423
■ **Open Hours:** 9:30–17:00 (Last entry at 16:30). Closed over the New Year's holiday and during distillery shutdowns.
■ **Website:** https://www.suntory.com/factory/yamazaki/

YOICHI DISTILLERY (HOKKAIDO)

The story of the Yoichi Distillery is very much the story of founder Masataka Taketsuru. In the beginning, Settsu Shuzo, an Osaka based company that Masataka worked for, invested in him as a researcher to venture to Scotland to learn all he could about making whisky. He went to Scotland in 1918 and enrolled at Glasgow University as a student in organic chemistry and while there became an apprentice at three distilleries. Upon returning to Japan, he learned that his job gave up its plan to make whisky due to recessions. That's when Shinjiro Torii, the founder of Kotobukiya Limited (present-day Suntory), hired Masataka in 1923 because he was the only one in Japan with the knowledge of how to distill whisky. Masataka was fundamental in the direct building of their Yamazaki Distillery, and he worked at Kotobukiya under contract for ten years. He left so he could create the archetype whisky of his dreams, and finally, in 1934, he founded the Yoichi Distillery.

The distillery location in the Yoichi district of Yoichi town, Hokkaido, was chosen because it was the place within Japan that most closely resembled that of Scotland. In 1936 the first pot still designed by Masataka and made in Japan was installed in Yoichi. In 1940 the first whisky from Nikka was released. The name of this first whisky line was "Nikka Whisky," an abbreviation of "Nippon Kaju," which later became the name of the company itself when it changed from "Dai Nippon Kaju." The Yoichi Distillery features six stills total, four wash, and two spirit stills.

■ **Address:** 〒046-0003 北海道余市郡余市町黒川町7丁目6
Hokkaido, Yoichi District, Yoichi, Kurokawacho, 7 Chome－6
〒046-0003
■ **Access:** About 70 minutes by train from Sapporo Station to Yoichi Station. By car 60 minutes.
■ **Tel:** 0135-23-3131
■ **Open Hours:** 9:00-17:00. There is a possibility the tour may be cancelled due to bad weather. During mid-winter some facilities cannot be observed.
■ **Website:** https://www.nikka.com/eng/distilleries/yoichi/

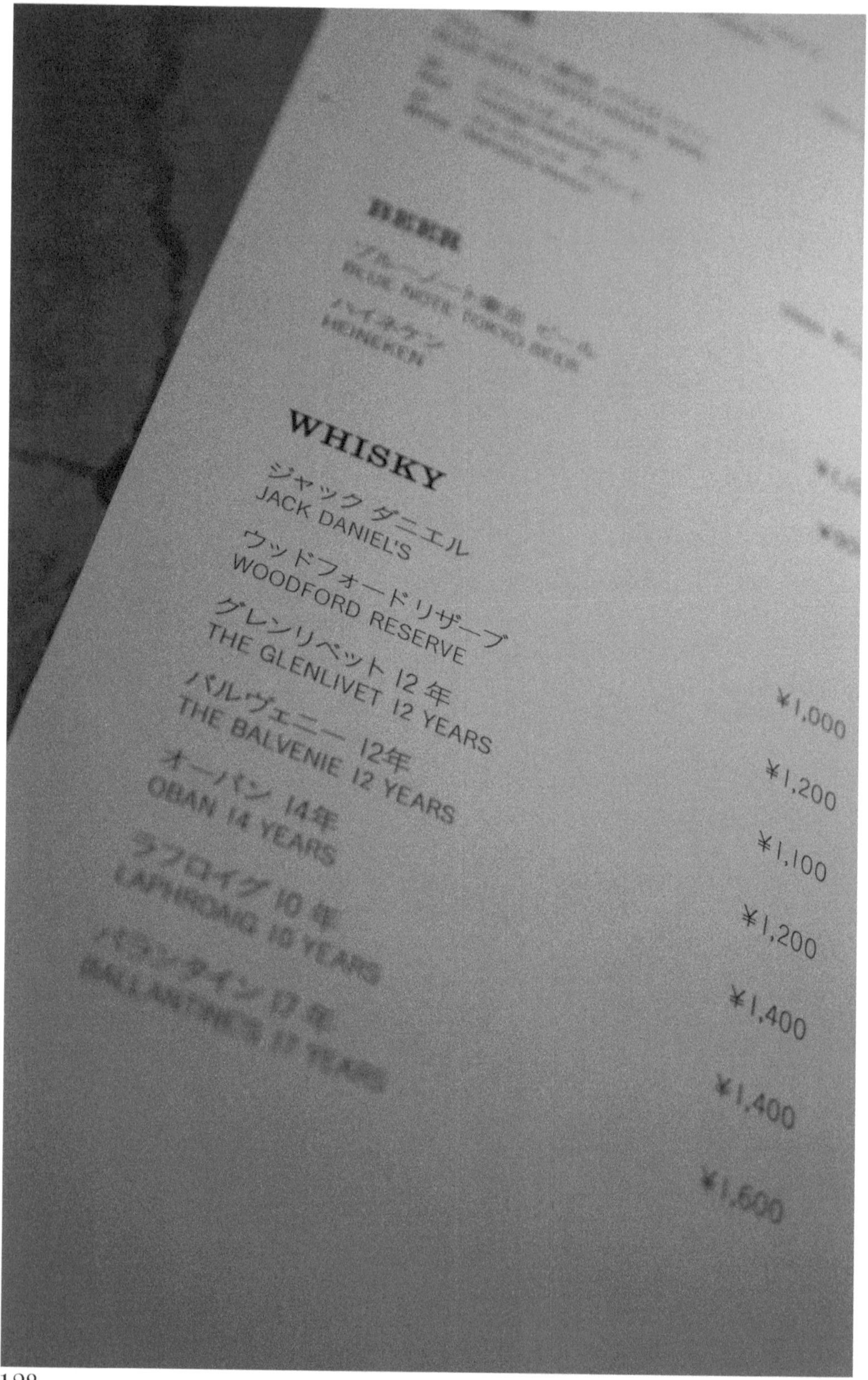

BEER

ブルーノート東京ビール
BLUE NOTE TOKYO BEER

ハイネケン
HEINEKEN

WHISKY

ジャック ダニエル
JACK DANIEL'S

ウッドフォード リザーブ
WOODFORD RESERVE

グレンリベット 12年
THE GLENLIVET 12 YEARS ¥1,000

バルヴェニー 12年
THE BALVENIE 12 YEARS ¥1,200

オーバン 14年
OBAN 14 YEARS ¥1,100

ラフロイグ 10年
LAPHROAIG 10 YEARS ¥1,200

バランタイン 17年
BALLANTINE'S 17 YEARS ¥1,400

¥1,400

¥1,600

THE *Bars*

82 ALE HOUSE (TOKYO)

HUB British Pub is a popular franchise throughout Japan (usually close to a train station). It features a British-style pub feel to it. It's very affordable, and it's highly popular with young adults. I would go so far as to say it's a pick-up spot for those hunting for the opposite sex. Additionally, whenever significant sporting events, matches, and games are taking place, you can usually watch them on the TVs here.

82 Ale House is also a pub-style establishment from the same owners as HUB, but it's a bit more upscale and classier than its counterpart. This is the place you go when you already have a significant other. Also, it's for the older demographic that just wants to go out for a cool one.

Both places have a complete ban on smoking now, have Wi-Fi, and accept credit cards. HUB has more beers, wines, and cocktails, while 82 Ale House has more whisky. They have about the same amount of spirits, albeit a little bit different. The food menu is generally the same at both, fish & chips, bite-size fish & chips, Margherita pizza, pasty, haggis, roast beef, and so on.

I do prefer 82 Ale House as I do consider myself a dandy man as well as a whisky man. The 82 Ale House I frequent is the one near Kinshicho Station, in the Sumida ward of Tokyo.

- **Address:** Lotte City Hotel Kinshicho 4F, 4-6-1, Kinshi, Sumida-ku, Tokyo 〒130-0013
(3 minute walk from the north exit of JR Kinshicho Station or subway.)
- **Tel:** 03-5619-8182
- **Open Hours:** Mon–Thu 17:00–0:30, Fri 17:00–2:00, Sat 16:00–2:00, Sun 15:00–0:00. Open 365 days a year.
- **Service Charge:** No service charge.
- **Website:** https://www.pub-hub.com/index.php/en

APOLLO (CHIBA)

Apollo is the sibling to Bar Memphis (which is also reviewed in this book). Whereas Memphis is an actual bar, Apollo is more of a restaurant. It is a more significant sized place with seating at the bar, dining tables, and tall round tables in the center of the room. It, like Memphis, is also located in Inage Ward, Chiba City. They are quite close, so close in fact that you can walk from one to the other in two minutes. And they are both a one minute walk from Inage Station.

Memphis is way more upscale in that the food is much more gourmet, tastier, and has a more abundance and variety of whiskies to choose from. With that quality naturally means the price is going to be more expensive than Apollo. But Apollo has its place with a more streamlined menu of drinks and food, and lower costs. The whiskies are going to be basic things such as your Jack Daniels Old No. 7, Maker's Mark, Canadian Club, Jameson, Johnnie Walker, Yamazaki NAS, etc. The food menu includes hamburgers and sliders, craft tacos, salad, soup, dessert, and more à la carte.

The atmosphere, although black-themed focus also, is different from that of Memphis, which is old-time jazz, soul, and blues. Apollo is a place of 90s R&B and hip hop. The venue also doubles as an event space for live music as it features a full stage with a piano, drums, microphones, etc. Monthly DJ events are standard too. I DJed there for opening night, New Year's Eve, Halloween, and other event dates.

- **Address:** King Arthur Karaoke 4F, 3-20-8 Inage Higashi, Inage-ku, Chiba-shi, Chiba 〒263-0031
(1 minute walk from JR Inage Station.)
- **Tel:** 043-307-9929
- **Open Hours:** Sun–Tue, Thu 18:00–02:00, Fri & Sat 18:00–03:00. Closed on Wednesday.
- **Service Charge:** No charge.
- **Website:** https://www.apollo-inage.com/
- **Instagram:** https://www.instagram.com/apollo_inage/

THE ARTY'S BAR / MOJITO LABORATORY (TOKYO)

The Arty's Bar was a place I frequented when I held my DJ residency at a downtown four-star hotel near Kita-Shinchi Station, Osaka. That's right, this bar used to be in downtown Osaka. When I left to go back to Tokyo in the fall of 2018, a year later, this bar closed its doors. Unbelievably in the month of publication of this book, I found out the bar master Atsushi, aka Arty, was reopening the bar in Ebisu, Tokyo! The opening date was Wednesday, July 15, 2020. I held off from sending this book to print just so that I could attend, catch the vibe, take the photo, and update this review.

Arty himself is a great mixer and a mojito specialist. He dubs himself a "mojito magician." The Arty's Bar is truly a spirits mixer bar, so first, you go for great mojitos, then daiquiris, then other cocktails. He also has a real refined selection of whiskies, rums, tequilas, gins, liqueurs, etc. Some whiskies that I reviewed, such as The Nikka 12 Years Old, were from here.

This bar has always been on a more different vibe than any other in Japan. It is very Generation X but feels very VIPish at the same time. Located only a minute walk away from Ebisu Station on the penthouse floor of the Barbizon bldg. It offers a great view of Shibuya's skyscrapers. The style is minimalistic and near the front, is what Arty calls a "Cuban style" secret room like a speakeasy. The background music is a smooth, chilled mix of adult contemporary R&B. Think Bobby Caldwell, and Deniece Williams "Free."

■ **Address:** Barbizon 105-8F, 4-4-15 Ebisu, Shibuya-ku, Tokyo 〒150-0013
(1 minute walk from the East Exit of JR Ebisu Station and Tokyo Metro Ebisu Station.)
■ **Tel:** 03-5860-2836
■ **Open Hours:** Mon—Thu 17:00—04:00, Fri, Sat 18:00—05:00, Closed Sunday and Holidays.
■ **Service Charge:** ¥1,000.

BAR MEMPHIS (CHIBA)

Bar Memphis since 2014. In my opinion, it is the best bar in Chiba Prefecture, and one of, if not the best bar in the Greater Tokyo Area. The bar is located in Inage Ward, one of the six wards of Chiba City, a one minute walk from Inage Station.

The reason I claim it to be the best is a culmination of things. Not in any particular order, but it's the service, food, music, atmosphere, and whisky selection. Although I never personally counted them, at a glance, I can tell Nao the bar owner has a stock of about 1000 records on deck. Ranging from blues to soul to jazz.

It is by far the best burger place in Greater Tokyo, I call the burgers "soul food burgers" because so much love and care goes into making them. I watch Nao make the buns from scratch each time I visit. The list of original hamburgers you can order is long, and all of them are delicious. Let me name a few and see if it whets your appetite. Avocado Cheese Burger, Double Cheese Burger, Mexican Chili Meat Burger, Wagyu Sirloin Steak Burger, Buffalo Chicken & Blue Cheese Burger, Honey Mustard Chicken Burger, all of those with craft beers, oh my!

Although all spirits are served, let's not forget this is primarily a whisky specialty bar. The bar master Nao is really a big fan of Scotches and knows how to select some popular ones along with limited editions and rarities. Your thirst will be quenched here.

- **Address:** Excellence Inage 2F, 3-8-13 Inage Higashi, Inage-ku, Chiba-shi, Chiba 〒263-0031
(1 minute walk from JR Inage Station.)
- **Tel:** 043-216-2735
- **Open Hours:** Sun–Thu 11:00–16:00, 17:00–01:00, Fri & Sat 11:00–16:00, 17:00–02:00. Closed on Tuesday.
- **Service Charge:** ¥300.
- **Website:** https://www.bar-memphis.com/
https://inage-bar-memphis.owst.jp/
- **Instagram:** https://www.instagram.com/memphis_inage/

BAR UK (OSAKA)

From the moment you walk through the front door and catch that first glimpse of the place, you know you're someplace special. You'll feel like you just found a gold mine. It's small, quaint, cozy, and stuffed to the brim with whisky. The bar master Eiji-san keeps it very well organized, neat, and clean. Located in downtown Osaka, you can enjoy various liquors of more than 400 bottles collected from all over the world here, but the focus is on the world whisky collection. The choices of Scotch whisky including old bottles from the '60s–'90s are a highlight, as well as the Japanese collection. For my research I've drank well over 50+ whiskies and taken over 150 photos in the span of 2 months here.

This is the kind of place that gives a guy like me goose bumps. The prices are the best you're going to get, with everything clearly noted on the bottles or menu. The bar itself is very atmospheric with the lighting, the cool art on the wall, and the jazz music in the background. It's a gentleman's bar and the real anchor that holds everything together is Eiji-san, an elder who is the proper textbook definition of a gentleman. I'm pleased to say you can rap with him in English or Japanese about whiskies, and he's very knowledgeable. This bar is a best of class, and my favorite in the entire country.

Bar UK is named by Ittetsu Narita (1949–2012): a famous paper-cutting artist known for great masterpieces of "bar scenes." There's a gallery displaying his original works inside the bar.

- **Address:** Ohkawa Bld. B1F 1-5-20 Sonezaki-shinichi, Kita-ku, Osaka 〒530-0002
(7 minute walk from JR Osaka Station or seconds walking from Kita-shinichi subway station.)
- **Tel:** 06-6342-0035
- **Open Hours:** Mon–Thu 16:00–22:30, Fri 16:00–23:00, Sat 14:00–20:30. Closed on Sunday, national holidays, and occasionally on Saturday or Wednesday.
- **Service Charge:** No service charge until 19:00. After ¥300.
- **Website:** https://www.facebook.com/arkwbaruk/

CABIN NAKAMEGURO (TOKYO)

In the Tokyo ward of Meguro, and upscale neighborhood of Nakameguro is where you can find this nice décor, posh and cozy spirits bar. Since this is not a whisky bar, you'll find a nice selection of all spirits and cocktails here. Apparently, they have good food too that I never knew about or tried because of my one-track mind.

My Brazilian friend Sullivan Gouvea with whom I use to train Brazilian jiu-jitsu with is the head bartender here. I found out about this place indirectly through his Instagram (@cabin_sullivan). Once he's been here for a while he slowly started turning his personal Instagram profile into one focused on Cabin and his bartending. The photos were all very well taken and made this establishment look so inviting. I've had it on my must-go list for the longest time, but once I finally made it, I was slapping myself silly wondering why I didn't come sooner.

While the shelves are not loaded with whisky, they have a curated selection of some higher-end ones and staples. Cabin's signature cocktails are great too. As Sullivan is a bonafide bartender, I put him to work by having him make me his top recommended drink for me, a negroni, and that's what I recommend to you all as well.

This is a cool groove kind of place, the kind of place you finish out date night with your trophy girlfriend on your arm. I must warn you however, you will be spending the coin for the experience.

- **Address:** 1-10-23 (Riverside Terrace 101) Naka-meguro, Meguro-Ku, Tokyo 〒153-0061
(6 minute walk From Naka-meguro Station.)
- **Tel:** 03-6303-2220
- **Open Hours:** Mon—Thu 19:00—late (around midnight). Friday & Saturday 19:00—02:00 (01:00 last order). Closed Sundays, national holidays, and the 1st and 3rd Monday of every month.
- **Service Charge:** No seating charge.
- **Website:** http://www.cabintokyo.com
- **Instagram:** https://www.instagram.com/cabin_nakameguro/

ONE SHOT BAR KEITH (OSAKA)

I never knew about this bar before it was recommended to me by bar master Eiji-san, the owner of Bar UK in Osaka. He told me that Keith has a lot of Chichibu whiskies and that I should check it out. While I prefer Bar UK, for it has a more extensive selection of age statements and rare Suntorys and Nikkas. Bar Keith has its niche with independent offerings. The Keith bar master Teruhiko Yamamoto has "carefully selected domestic whiskies from general items to limited items." Bar Keith has the largest selection of Ichiro's, rare and expensive Akashis, a large Nikka selection, and some high aged Suntorys. So for its Japanese inventory, it's one of the best in the country.

The premise of the shop is that the owner wanted to open a place in a neighborhood of the city where people who live there would drop in often. "I want to make a restaurant where mothers can take their children and have a casual meal." This is one of the best bars you can go to in terms of Japanese whiskies. I could have found myself going there more often had the prices been more affordable. Little did I know they are affordable, I just went at the wrong time without having any foreknowledge. I went there with intentions of drinking rare whisky, knowing it was going to be expensive, but I didn't know about the happy hour system in place there. *Customers visiting between 17:00 and 19:00 don't have to pay the ¥500 seating charge that customers coming after 19:00 have to pay. Also, the drinks are 50% off (excluding some whiskies).

- **Address:** 2-14-1 Miyahara, Yodogawa-Ku, Osaka 〒532-0003 (8 minute walk From JR Shin-Osaka Station Exit 1.)
- **Tel:** 06-6393-0170
- **Open Hours:** Wed–Mon 17:00–24:00. Closed on Tuesdays.
- **Service Charge:** No charge between 17:00–19:00. *A ¥500 charge will be charged for stays after 19:00, and for customers entering after 19:00.
- **Website:** http://www.bar-keith.com/

STARBUCKS RESERVE ROASTERY TOKYO

The Starbucks Reserve Roastery Tokyo opened Thursday, February 28, 2019. It was the world's largest Starbucks until the 35,000 square feet Chicago Roastery opened and took the number one spot in November that same year. Four floors of exclusive drinks. Going up. On the first floor is the main bar, and this is where they serve coffee. This is not just any old coffee, or the same stuff you get at any old Starbucks. This is what Starbucks deems to be the best beans they find from around the world, and prices really reflect that as the Starbucks Reserve is not for the faint of pocket. On the second floor is all teas. The third floor is all cocktails and alcoholic mix drinks, many featuring coffee in them. And the fourth floor is the lounge with additional seating and tables.

Our focus today is on the third floor, called Arriviamo Bar. Here unique liquor cocktails are made, and many featuring coffee and liquor are concocted. On opening day, I had the Sparkling Sakura Allure for ¥2,000. It's labeled "Tropical and floral tea paired with a light whisky for a nuanced sparkling beverage showcasing the lighter side of whisky and darker side of tea." This is one of two drinks on the menu that contain whisky. It features Suntory Chita Single Grain Whisky. On a subsequent visit, I had the second drink infused with whisky, the Tokyo Pour-Over. It is the most expensive drink on the menu at ¥3,000. "The signature pour-over cocktail is served from a chilled sake carafe, into small sake glasses. Great for one or to share." It features Mars Iwai Tradition Blended Japanese Whisky.

- **Address:** 2-19-23 Aobadai, Meguro-ku, Tokyo 〒153-0042 (11 minute walk from Naka-meguro Station.)
- **Tel:** 03-6417-0202
- **Open Hours:** Sun—Sat 07:00—23:00.
- **Service Charge:** None.
- **Website:** https://www.starbucks.co.jp/reserve/roastery/
- **Instagram:** https://www.instagram.com/starbucksreserve_tokyo/

TOKYO WHISKY LIBRARY (TOKYO)

This bar/restaurant opened its doors on October 3, 2016 and is located just a 1-minute walk away from Omotesando Station in Minami-Aoyama, Tokyo, an upscale neighborhood of Shibuya ward that features high cost living along with designer boutique stores. It seems obviously inspired by the Brandy Library in TriBeCa downtown Lower Manhattan, New York City to me, and for a place that opened 12 years after, you might be expecting something bigger and better. To me it feels smaller, and it's definitely not as atmospheric as the Brandy Library, which oozes personality, originality, and is the pinnacle in social bars.

I felt a bit disappointed after walking through those doors late night on November 12, 2018. The place just didn't meet my mental expectations, but what did I expect exactly? For what it's supposed to be I was expecting not only the best bar in Tokyo, but also in Japan. And with a name like Tokyo Whisky Library I was also expecting a flagship whisky bar for the country that showcased none other than Japanese whiskies. Unfortunately their limited range of Japanese whiskies left me entirely unsatisfied.

Bar UK in Osaka has not only more Japanese whiskies, but also a better curated selection of both Japanese and international whiskies. Cabin Nakameguro feels cozier, moodier, and more intimate. Don't get me wrong, this is a nice bar because it has a varied array of whiskies, just other bars are better at other things than this is.

- **Address:** Minamiaoyama Santakiarakyoukai 2F, 5-5-24, Minamiaoyama, Minato-ku, Tokyo 〒107-0062 (1 minute walk From Omotesando Station, Exit B3. Accessible from the Tokyo Metro Ginza Line, Hanzomon Line, and Chiyoda Line.)
- **Tel:** 03-6434-1163
- **Open Hours:** Mon–Fri 18:00–27:00 (Last call at 26:00), Sat 15:00–27:00 (Last call at 26:00), Sun 15:00–24:00.
- **Service Charge:** 10%.
- **Website:** http://www.tokyo-whisky-library.com
- **Instagram:** https://www.instagram.com/tokyowhiskylibrary/

上段（左から右）

- スコットランド ウイスキー・ツーリズム
- THE WHISKY CATALOG & BIBLE ウイスキーの教科書　橋口孝司
- いちばんよくわかる ウイスキーの教室　山下大知 著　The most understandable lecture on whisky　Text by Daichi Yamashita
- ビジネスとしてのウイスキー
  - なぜ今、高級ウイスキーが2億円で売れるのか
  - ワインを超える投資対象になるのか？
  - ジャパニーズウイスキーに外国人が熱狂するのはなぜ？
  - これから絶対に飲みたい幻の蒸溜所はどこか？
  - 空前の大ブームの真相　世界的に知られ

下段（左から右）

- シングルモルト&ウイスキー シリーズ30万部突破　ナツメ社
- ウイスキー完全バイブル　土屋守　ナツメ社
- 新版 ウイスキー検定 公式テキスト　土屋守＝執筆・監修　小学館
- ウイスキー&シングルモルト完全ガイド　PAMPERO編著　小学館
- 伝説と呼ばれる 至高のウイスキー101　イアン・バクストン　スチュアート・ヴィン・エイケン　田岡明美 訳　土屋守 日本語版監修　WAVE出版
- ジャパニーズ・ウイスキーと蒸溜所ガイド決定版　ウイスキー・ライジング　Whisky Rising　小学館
- 101 Legendary Whiskies
- DK 改訂 世界ウイスキー大図鑑　チャールズ・マクリーン　柴田書店
- 世界のウイスキー図鑑　デイヴ・ブルーム　GAIA BOOKS
- 世界が認めた日本のウイスキー　橋口孝司　清水亮 他　X-Knowledge
- ウイスキーブック　SCOTCH WHISKY IRISH JAPANESE WHISKY AMERICAN WHISKY CRAFT WHISKY OLD MUSIC GEAR etc.
- ウイスキー学 メジャーからクラフトまで　ドミニク・ロスクロウ

148

THE *Books*

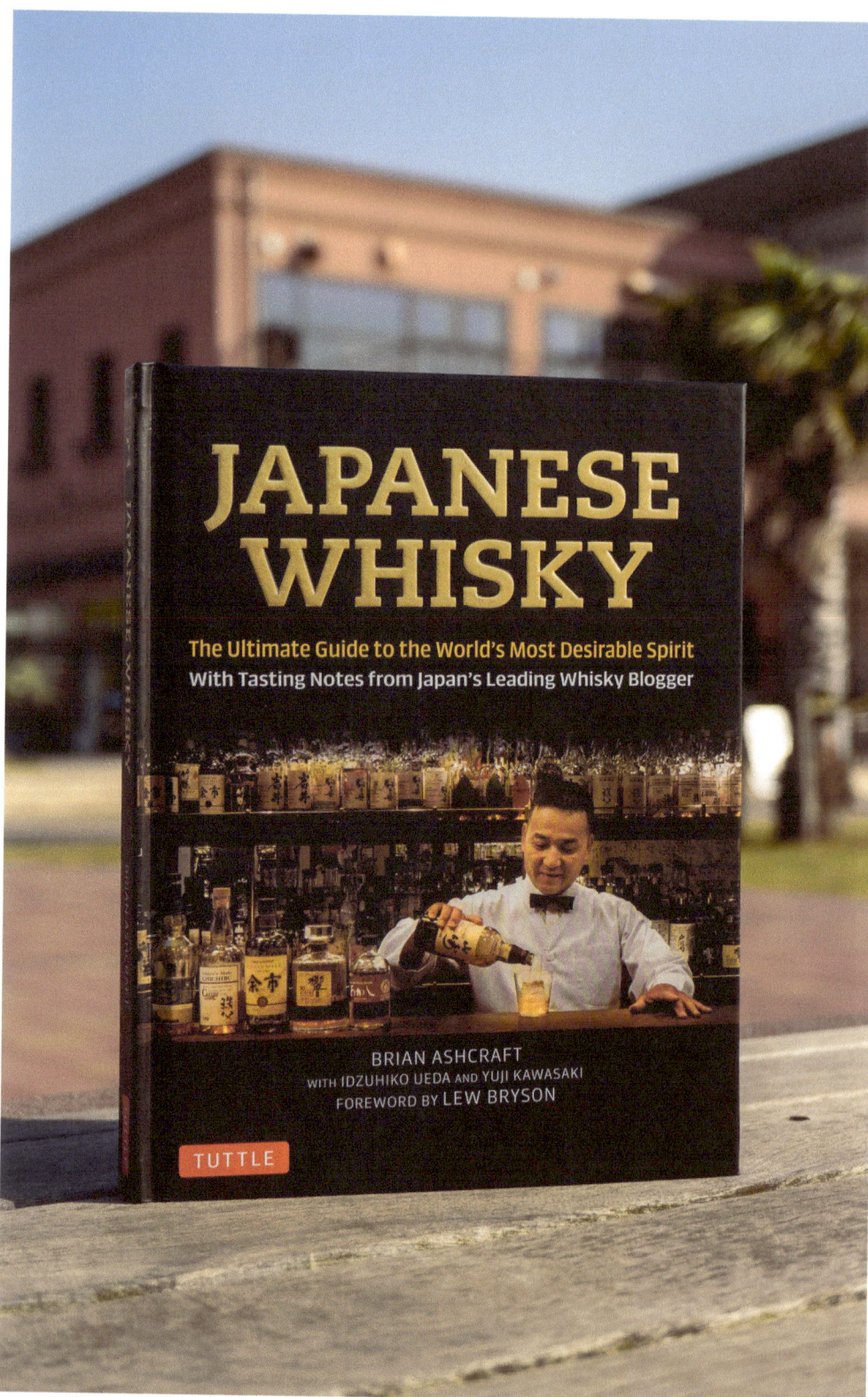

JAPANESE WHISKY

On the cover of the book is the tagline that reads, "The Ultimate Guide to the World's Most Desirable Spirit." It's hardly the definitive guide, it's just the latest guide. I would call this the fourth book out on the topic of Japanese whisky, coming out only two years before my own. What I like most about it is its well organized, and its accessibility. It's way cheaper to acquire than the other books in this section, and it's a shorter read making it easier to get into, but there is a caveat with that. Being shorter does make it less in-depth.

The photos and images selected and used in this book are certainly a lot more archival and stock than say the original ones featured in "Whisky Japan" or "The Way of Whisky." I'm going to leave it up to your interpretation of whether you think that is a good or bad thing. For me, I've seen most of these photos and images when I visited the distilleries here in Japan, when I visit the distillers' websites, and when I flip through their pamphlets, etc. The ones in "Whisky Japan," while they look a lot less historical, are more original. I suppose both have their place.

The biggest issue I have with this book is that it feels like the fourth dipping of things already said. This hits all the basic beats you'd expect with books on the subject matter: the history of Japanese whisky, a look at the distilleries of Japan, and brief tasting notes. Nothing here is really groundbreaking.

- ■ **Author:** Brian Ashcraft with Idzuhiko Ueda and Yuji Kawasaki. Foreword by Lew Bryson
- ■ **Publisher:** Tuttle Publishing
- ■ **ISBN:** 9784805314098
- ■ **Format:** Hardcover
- ■ **Year:** May 29, 2018
- ■ **Pages:** 144
- ■ **US Price:** $19.99
- ■ **Japan Price:** ¥2,200

THE WAY OF WHISKY

Let me say at the outset. This book is a memoir and reads utterly different from the others I reviewed. It's more a narrative diary on Japan than a hardcore whisky book. But if you're into Japanese culture or a Japanophile, this is undoubtedly for you.

When I opened this book and saw the author sitting half-lotus style on an old wood floor in front of a shōji screen and doors, I knew almost immediately what I wasn't going to like about it. The book tries too hard to go out of its way to be intentionally Japanese by using as many forced tropes and Japanese words as possible (shinkansen, maiko, shokunin, kaizen, haiku). The glossary has many unassociated beginner Japanese as well. There's just no correlation with whisky, and it feels so cliché. But I get it, visitors to Japan are so caught up and enamored by feeling, author Dave Broom probably just wanted to express what he felt. I just don't like how it's done. Criticisms aside, it was a decent book. It was an engaging, easy flowing read apart from those parts. I also liked the photography by Kohei Take. The photos are beautifully taken and feature deep contrast in their washed-out style.

Finally, I think the book could have been organized a little better. The categorial green pages (you'll understand when you read it) should have been grouped together, and the whisky reviews grouped together. Instead, they are spliced in with the core writing (the journal), breaking up the flow. An odd editorial choice I feel.

- **Author:** Dave Broom, Photography by Kohei Take
- **Publisher:** Mitchell Beazley
- **ISBN:** 9781784723958
- **Format:** Hardcover, eBook
- **Year:** October 5, 2017
- **Pages:** 256
- **US Price:** $50.00
- **Japan Price:** ¥9,200

WHISKY JAPAN

Author Dominic Roskrow is an efficient, to the point writer. In his book's nail on the head introduction, he concisely wraps up Japanese whisky affairs in 2020, even though his book came out in 2016. He's the first author on the subject matter. He spoke on such issues as the influence of Scottish whisky, and Japan going its own way. The severe problem of Japan importing malt whisky from Scotland and how many commentators (me included) suggesting that the practice is wrong. He talks about everything from its history to making, looking at distilleries, tasting notes, bar showcases, etc. No matter how differently future authors tried to make their books. They'll each have some writing styles, topics, themes, or categories that are a double-dipping of what was found in this book. It's all subjective to the reader, but to me, this is arguably the best one.

Roskrow himself considers his book "a work of investigative journalism" and not a "techie" book on Japanese whisky (page 20). In a recent interview that premiered on May 2, 2020, on a YouTube video titled Japanese Whisky Lockdown: Episode 4. In his own words, Roskrow said, "There are two ways you can write a book. You can write a book as an expert. I guess I am an expert and I'm telling you. Or you can do it as a journalist and say, I'm not an expert, but I can go out and talk to the people who are. And so that's what I did in this book. I basically took a subject and asked a question. How did it go from nowhere to everywhere? From zero to hero." Dominic indeed covers it all and leaves no stone unturned.

- **Author:** Dominic Roskrow , Foreword by Mike Miyamoto
- **Publisher:** Kodansha USA
- **ISBN:** 9781568365756
- **Format:** Hardcover
- **Year:** October 1, 2016
- **Pages:** 288
- **US Price:** $34.95
- **Japan Price:** ¥4,900 before tax

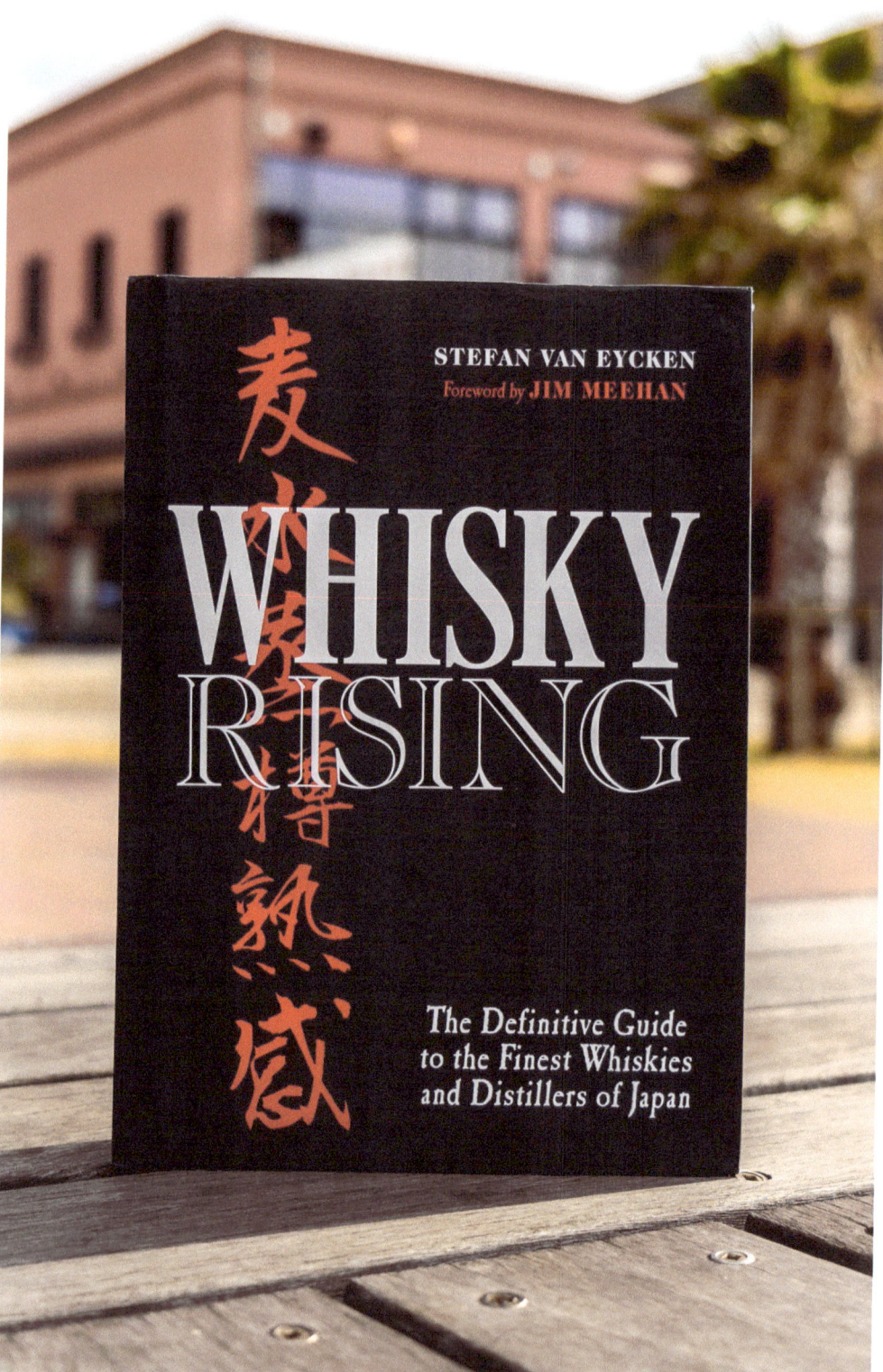

WHISKY RISING

This is the most thorough book in the lot of the four released. It spans everything from history to distillery and bar visits, and a look at numbers, statistics, and information. The photos are mostly original, but it features a few stock images of critical people and advertisements.

Split into three parts, part one chronicles the history of Japanese whisky and product releases in chronological order. Presentation-wise, thematically, and graphically the information is very well laid out and presented. There are a lot of charts, graphs, and tables presenting essential data. Such as sales numbers, taxation information, bottle prices and sizes, whisky market shares by manufacturer, Japanese whisky consumption by years, awards, price comparisons, etc. Part two showcases Japanese distilleries of the past and present, and profiles the major players of master blenders for each one. Twenty four unique distilleries are presented, whether they are still operational or defunct. Part three is bar listings and whisky reviews.

My criticisms. The original photos are not as beautiful as the ones in other books. They get the job done, even if they lack elegance. But I could say my 2018 Samsung Galaxy S9+ smartphone could probably take better quality photographs than a lot of what I saw here. The whisky reviews are entirely out of touch, showing only very old & rare unaffordable whiskies.

- **Author:** Stefan Van Eycken, Foreword by Jim Meehan
- **Publisher:** Cider Mill Press
- **ISBN:** 9781604336979
- **Format:** Hardcover
- **Year:** April 4, 2017
- **Pages:** 400
- **US Price:** $35.00
- **Japan Price:** ¥4,116

Honorable Mention

KAVALAN CLASSIC SINGLE MALT WHISKY

Captain's Log, Stardate 2018.10.21. This single malt is from the 2005 newly founded, first whisky distillery of Taiwan just south of Taipei. Newsflash! Even though this is a book about Japanese whiskies, Taiwan is now the only place other than Japan in East Asia that makes whisky. The inclusion in this book is honorary. With three main series lines (Kavalan, Solist, and Premium) that should theoretically get better in quality and more expensive, the higher up you move through them. Here is a whisky from the most basic line.

I managed to get lucky and find a miniature of this along with two other Kavalan line whiskies at an Aeon supermarket in Chiba City, sometime in December 2017. I finally got around to tasting them during my five-month stay in Osaka in September 2018.

It's a proper and adequate all-around single malt, but one that plays it very safe. I want something more from it. I kept seeing the word "complexity" all over the box, but it isn't so much. I want something that takes chances, more dangerous, so to speak. It's not better than it's two brothers I tried (Kavalan Concertmaster Port Cask Finish, and ex-Bourbon Oak). My verdict is it seems overpriced for what is offered. Maybe more expensive in Japan than elsewhere. I can empathize now with those in America who buy Japanese whisky.

- **Nose:** Pleasant and fruity. Mangos, vanilla in the backdrop.
- **Palate:** Extremely light, a little oily. A light taste of mangos.
- **Finish:** The intensity of the taste of mangos increases with swallowing, a little buttery.
- **Color:** Lively and passionate amber.
- **ABV:** 40%.
- **Distillery:** Kavalan, aka King Car.
- **Price:** ¥13,750 tax included (700ml).

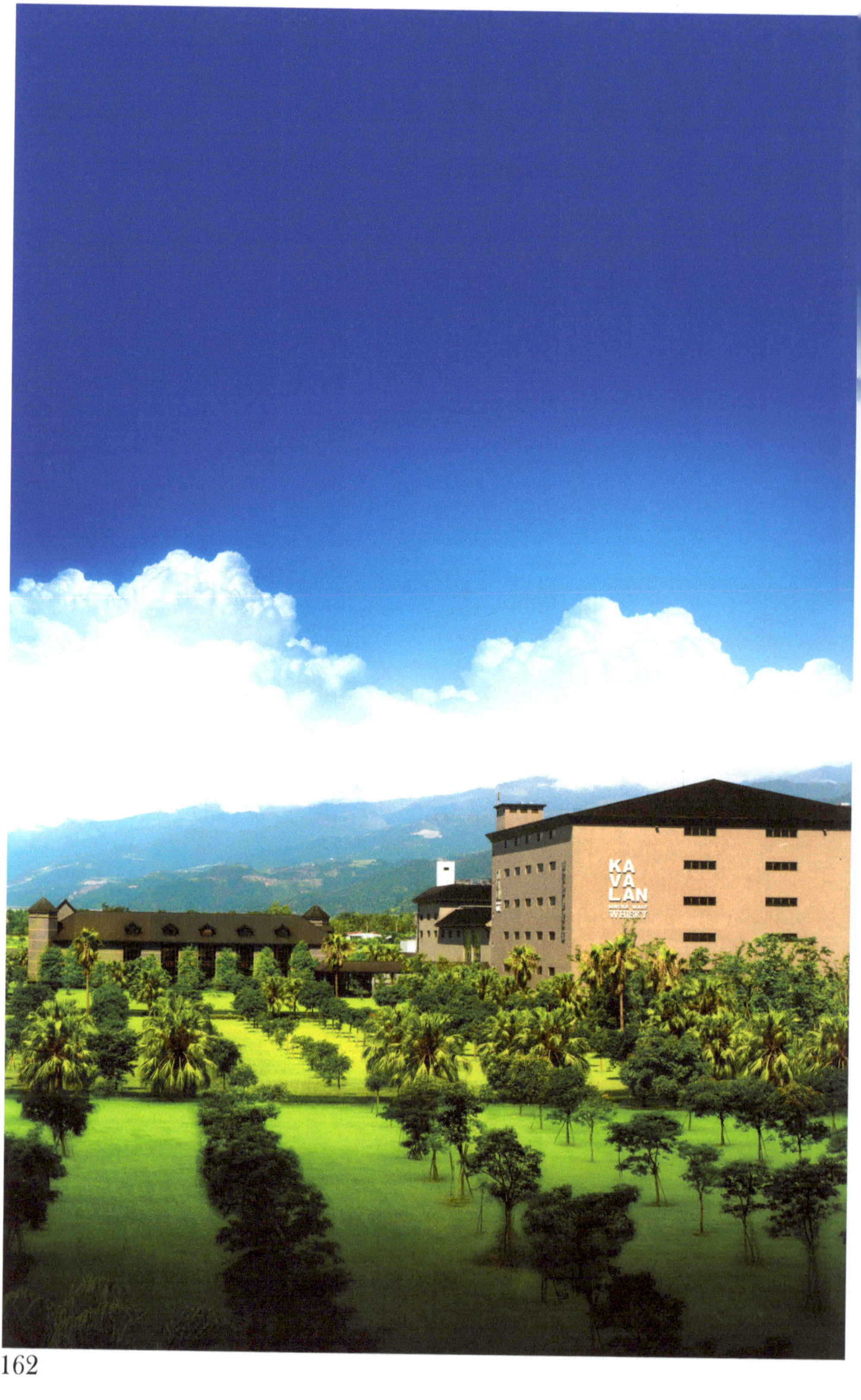
KA
VA
LAN
WHISKY

KING KAR KAVALAN (TAIWAN)

Having completed construction on New Year's Eve in 2005, the Kavalan Distillery opened its doors to the public three years after and released its first single malt whisky in 2008. Kavalan is named after the indigenous people of Taiwan who inhabited the plain that is modern-day Yilan County. It is there, just southeast of Taipei, but in the northern part of the country where the distillery is located. The region's weather features a temperate, no dry season, hot summer (Cfa), and the surrounding mountain region is temperate. So unlike the cold climates of Scotland and even Japan in which whisky matures rather slowly, maturation occurs much more rapidly at Kavalan. Like all distilleries anywhere in the world, you always need high-quality water to make your whisky with. Kavalan uses the mineral waters from the nearby mountain.

From the outside, Kavalan has a very striking appearance. Many large buildings are interconnected, and the outward appearance is a modern one. It's the most modern-looking distillery that I've ever laid eyes on. Founder and entrepreneur, Mr. Tien-Tsai Lee's determination, was to make world-class whiskies here that could compete with those of Scotland and Japan. They went on to become a line of premium whiskies challenging the world's best.

Kavalan is given honorable mention in this book because, aside from all the distilleries within Japan, it's the only one within East Asia.

■ **Address:** 宜蘭縣員山鄉員山路2段326號
326, Section 2, Yuan-shan Road, Yuan-Shan, Yi-Lan, Taiwan. 26444
■ **Access:** Bus: Kamalan Bus / Kuo-Kuang Bus.
Taxi: From Yilan railway station or Yilan Transfer Station, it costs about NTD$250 to NTD$300, for a 15 to 20 minute journey.
■ **Tel:** (03) 9229-000#1104
■ **Open Hours:** 09:00—18:00 Open all-year-round. On Lunar New Year's Eve the venue closes early at 5.00pm.
■ **Website:** http://www.kavalanwhisky.com/en

BAR BACKYARD (TOKYO)

Blue Note Tokyo is, by far, Japan's best jazz club and one of the finest establishments for the genre the world over. In the B1 lobby, there is a bar called Backyard. You can have drinks in the actual club itself, so why is it there? Its reason for being is it's a place where you can have an aperitif before the performance and again after the show. And also, you don't have to be a ticket holder or going to attend a show to go to this bar. It's open to all customers, even those just simply wanting to drink at the bar. It's a rather small, but nice and cool space featuring a charming décor and air about it.

It has a streamlined menu featuring the usual champagne, house wine, a couple of beers, a few cocktails, soft drinks, coffee & tea. But the whisky menu. Surprisingly they don't have any Japanese whiskies on the menu*, but I think they should. Because of that little asterisk mark, I can only give them an honorary mention for bars. Hopefully, that will change soon.

- **Address:** 6-3-16, Minamiaoyama, Minato-ku, Tokyo 〒107-0062 (8 minute walk from Tokyo Metro Omotesando Station.)
- **Tel:** 03-5485-0790
- **Open Hours:** Mon–Fri 17:00–23:00 (Last order), Sat., Sun & Holiday 15:30–22:00 (Last order). Hours are subject to change due to the show schedule at Blue Note Tokyo.
- **Service Charge:** Admission free.
- **Website:** https://www.bar-backyard.com/

BRANDY LIBRARY (NEW YORK CITY)

The best place to drink whisky outside Japan. Open since 2004, the Brandy Library is the quintessential cosmopolitan metropolitan bar. Located in the TriBeCa (Triangle Below Canal Street), New York City neighborhood of Manhattan, it's where you dream about going to when you're thinking of a big night out on the town. Better bring your gold card because it's about to get expensive.

A few years back, a manager told me that the owner, Frenchman Flavien Desoblin, thought Cognac/brandy was going to be the next big thing in spirits. So he named the place what it is. It turns out whisky was the one that was set to blow up big and thrive.

There are hundreds of brown spirits to choose from here. Rough estimates at a glance, it looks like near 400 kinds of brandy and over 600 unique offerings of whisky from around the world, and that's just what's listed on the menu. I'm sure rarities come in all the time that are not even written in permanently that you have to inquire about. Then you have your rums, tequilas, and mezcals. It's the most extensive spirits menu I've encountered anywhere personally.

Then there's the icing on the cake, distillers, master blenders, sommeliers, and such come in regularly to give presentations and do tastings with clientele. Of mention, although I didn't review it, as I've never been. There is a second bar Copper & Oak also in NYC on the Lower East Side, from the same owner. It's worth a visit.

- **Address:** 25 N Moore St, New York, NY 10013
- **Tel:** (212) 226-5545
- **Open Hours:** Sun—Wed 17:00—01:00, Thu 16:00—02:00 01:00, Fri & Sat 16:00—04:00.
- **Website:** http://brandylibrary.com/
- **Instagram:** https://www.instagram.com/brandylibrarynyc/

Bibliography

BIBLIOGRAPHY

Akashi Red Blended Whisky. Products: Whisky: Akashi Red Blended Whisky. http://www.tokinosakagura.com/product/akashi-red-blended-whisky/ (1 Oct 2018)

Chita Distillery. Suntory: Global: Distilleries: Chita. https://whisky.suntory.com/en/global/distilleries/chita

Chivas Regal Mizunara. コレクション: Chivas Regal Mizunara. https://www.chivas.com/ja-JP/our-collection/chivas-mizunara (1 Oct 2018)

Eigashima Shuzo. Producers: Eigashima Shuzo. http://www.tokinosakagura.com/team/eigashima/ (1 Oct 2018)

About Fuji Gotemba Distillery. トップ: 商品情報: ウイスキー・ブランデー: 富士御殿場蒸溜所: 富士御殿場蒸溜所について. https://www.kirin.co.jp/products/whisky_brandy/gotemba/care/index.html (26 Apr 2020)

Hakushu Distillery. Suntory: Global: Distilleries: Hakushu. https://whisky.suntory.com/en/global/distilleries/hakushu

Hanyu Distillery (Closed). Whisky Magazine Japan. http://whiskymag.jp/hanyu-distillery/ (1 Oct 2018)

Hibiki – bottled around 1990. Whisky Saga. http://www.whiskysaga.com/blog/hibiki-bottled-around-1990 (2 Jun 2019)

The History of Ichiro's Malt whisky, and the Chichibu Distillery Tour. Fun! Chichibu. https://fun-chichibu.com/en/10742/ (1 Oct 2018)

BIBLIOGRAPHY

Ichiro Akuto: Japanese Whisky's Rock Star. Whiskycast. https://whiskycast.com/ichiro-akuto-japanese-whiskys-rock-star/ (25 Jan 2020)

Japanese whisky boom leads to shortage. NHK WORLD: News: Backstories – the facts behind the news. https://www3.nhk.or.jp/nhkworld/nhknewsline/backstories/japanesewhisky/ (10 Mar 2019)

Kavalan. Story: About Kavalan. http://www.kavalanwhisky.com/en/story-about.aspx (24 Sep 2018)

Kavalan Classic Single Malt Whisky. Whisky: Kavalan Series. http://www.kavalanwhisky.com/en/product-detailed.aspx?Serno=19# (24 Sep 2018)

Kirin Corporate Overview. Kirin: Corporate Profile: Corporate Overview. https://www.kirinholdings.co.jp/english/company/overview/index.html (26 Apr 2020)

Kirin Corporate History. Kirin: Corporate Profile: Corporate History (1885-1989). https://www.kirinholdings.co.jp/english/company/overview/index.html (26 Apr 2020)

Kirin Fuji-Sanroku Signature Blend. キリン公式オンライン通販 DRINX: ウイスキー: 富士山麓: キリンウイスキー 富士山麓 Signature Blend. https://drinx.kirin.co.jp/whisky/fs/fssignature2/ (8 Mar 2019)

BIBLIOGRAPHY

Kirin Pure Malt Whisky. キリン公式オンライン通販DRINX: ウイスキー: 富士御殿場蒸溜所: 富士御殿場蒸溜所 ピュアモルトウイスキー (Kirin Official Online Mail Order DRINX: Whisky: Fuji Gotemba Distillery: Fuji Gotemba Distillery Pure Malt Whisky). https://drinx.kirin.co.jp/whisky/fg/puremalt2/ (8 Mar 2019)

Miyagikyo Distillery. Nikka: The Distilleries: Miyagikyo Distillery. https://www.nikka.com/eng/distilleries/miyagikyo/ (28 Dec 2019)

BLACK HISTORY. ブラックニッカ: 商品紹介: NIKKA WHISKY: NIKKA WHISKY. https://www.nikka.com/products/blended/blacknikka/history.html#y2015 (24 Sep 2018)

Nikka Black Rich Blend. Nikka: Products: Blended: Black Rich. https://www.nikka.com/products/blended/blackrich/ (26 Dec 2019)

Nikka Coffey Grain Whisky. Nikka: Products: Grain Whisky. https://www.nikka.com/eng/products/grain/coffeygrain.html (24 Sep 2018)

Nikka Coffey Malt Whisky. Nikka: Products: Grain Whisky. https://www.nikka.com/eng/products/grain/coffeymalt.html (24 Sep 2018)

Nikka Taketsuru Pure Malt 17 Years Old. Nikka: Products: Pure Malt (Blended Malt) https://www.nikka.com/eng/products/pure-malt/taketsuru.html (24 Sep 2018)

BIBLIOGRAPHY

Nikka The Nikka 12 Years Old. Nikka: Products: Blended. https://www.nikka.com/eng/products/blended/thenikka12.html (24 Sep 2018)

Nikka Whisky Date. トップ: 商品紹介: ブレンデッドウイスキー: 伊達 (Nikka: Products: Blended: Date). https://www.nikka.com/products/blended/date/index.html (28 Dec 2019)

Nikka Whisky Single Malt Miyagikyo. Nikka: Products: Single Malt. https://www.nikka.com/eng/products/single-malt/miyagikyo.html (24 Sep 2018)

Nikka Whisky Single Malt Yoichi. Nikka: Products: Single Malt. https://www.nikka.com/eng/products/single-malt/yoichi.html (24 Sep 2018)

Nikka Whisky Super Nikka. Nikka: Products: Blended. https://www.nikka.com/eng/products/blended/super.html (24 Sep 2018)

Not All 'Japanese Whisky' Is Japanese Whisky. Home: Magazine: Features: Features: Not All 'Japanese Whisky' Is Japanese Whisky. https://scotchwhisky.com/magazine/features/19680/not-all-japanese-whisky-is-japanese-whisky/ (7 Jan 2020)

The Origin Of Yamazaki. Products: Yamazaki: The Origin. https://whisky.suntory.com/en/global/products/yamazaki/the-origin (12 May 2020)

BIBLIOGRAPHY

Some Japanese Whiskies Aren't From Japan. Some Aren't Even Whisky. Homepage: Food.
https://www.nytimes.com/2020/05/29/dining/japanese-whisky.html (30 May 2020)

サントリーウイスキー 響 *1990年代流通 43% 第2期ボトル* *(Suntory Whisky Hibiki circulation in the 1990s 43% second period bottle).* http://whiskywarehouse.blog.jp/archives/1063502834.html (2 Jun 2019)

Suntory unveils its first-ever world blended whisky, Suntory World Whisky 'Ao.' Suntory: Newsroom: News Release: Suntory unveils its first-ever world blended whisky, Suntory World Whisky 'Ao.' https://www.suntory.com/news/article/13360E.html (6 May 2020)

刻の酒蔵 *Toki No Sakagura.* ウイスキー蒸留所.
http://www.ei-sake.jp/all/distillery.html (1 Oct 2018)

Torys Suntory Whisky. Product: Whisky: Suntory Whisky Torys: Torys Classic: Brand Site.
https://www.suntory.co.jp/whisky/torys/classic/ (7 Jan 2020)

Torys Honey, a whisky-based liqueur, will be launched for a limited time.
https://www.suntory.co.jp/news/2012/11496.html (7 Jan 2020)

White Oak Akashi Blended Whisky. Products: Whisky: Page 2: White Oak Akashi Blended Whisky
http://www.tokinosakagura.com/product/akashi-white/ (1 Oct 2018)

BIBLIOGRAPHY

White Oak Akashi Single Malt Whisky. Products: Whisky: Page 2: White Oak Akashi Single Malt Whisky http://www.tokinosakagura.com/product/akashi-single-malt-whisky/ (1 Oct 2018)

Yamanashi Sake and Shochu Makers Association. SanFoods. http://www.yamanashi-sake.jp/en/brewery/sanfoods/ (1 Oct 2018)

Yamazaki. Suntory: Brands: Spirits: Yamazaki. https://www.suntory.com/brands/yamazakisinglemaltwhisky/ (20 May 2020)

Yamazaki Distillery. Suntory: Global: Distilleries: Yamazaki. https://whisky.suntory.com/en/global/distilleries/yamazaki (20 May 2020)

Yoichi Distillery. Nikka: The Distilleries: Yoichi Distillery. https://www.nikka.com/eng/distilleries/yoichi/ (28 Dec 2019)

ABOUT THE AUTHOR

Marc Antomattei |'an tō mat tā| was born in El Paso, Texas, on January 4, 1983. Marc is the youngest of four brothers. His Puerto Rican father, Augustin Antomattei from New York City, was a serviceman in the US Army. His African-American mother, Dorothy Antomattei (née Sims) from Waco, Texas, was a homemaker.

Upon reaching adulthood, Marc enlisted in US Air Force, where on July 31, 2003, he arrived in the Greater Tokyo Area as a serviceman. After being honorably discharged in February 2006, Antomattei remained in Japan. He currently works as a professional DJ, freelance graphic designer, writer, and teacher.

Stay in touch with Marc Antomattei by friending him on these various social sites:

Facebook: www.facebook.com/marc.antomattei
LinkedIn: https://www.linkedin.com/in/marcantomattei
YouTube: htttps://www.youtube.com/gentlemanmasterclass
Email: marcantomatteiproductions@gmail.com

This book is supported by Gentleman Masterclass and Gentleman's Club WHISKY. Follow them on social media at

YouTube: Gentleman's Club WHISKY
Instagram: @gentlemansclubwhisky
Twitter: @GentlemanWhisky
Facebook: @gentlemansclubwhisky
Email: gentlemansclubwhisky@gmail.com

The mountain range that overlooks the Hakushu Distillery.

Epilogue

EPILOGUE

I humble myself. Thank you all for your support. This book was both a passion project and me seizing an opportunity. At the same time, I have put in the work and submitted much time and money into the craft we call tasting reviews. If I had lived in the UK, this book could have easily been *50 Scotches*, or in America, *50 Bourbons*.

I consider the 50 recommendations I selected for this book to be whiskies for real people. Most are within reach to find, within reason to buy, and that's why I chose them. Despite prices for the more substantial Japanese whiskies being relatively higher than from other regions of the world, you are generally getting pretty good if not distinctive whiskies and wonderful individual experiences. This is the game we pay to play. As Japanese whisky is the talk of the town, if you want to participate in the conversation and be a part of the global trend at the time it's happening, you have to drink it.

Ultimately, I'm personally glad I took the journey to go down this road. To become acquainted with this abundance of Japanese whiskies, gain some insight into them, and come away with understanding and knowledge, it's gratifying. It's not something many can attest to being able to do or have done. It feels good to say your experiences expand beyond the typical, usual Hibiki and Yamazaki and assert yourself as an expert on it.

I would like to tell you that this is just the start of our journey together. I plan to write more in this genre, and I hope that as a reader, you'd be willing to join me again. I think we are all ready to graduate to the next level together. Hopefully, I can make my future works more prominent than the first. With your support, of course. Kanpai!

www.ingramcontent.com/pod-product-compliance
Lightning Source LLC
Chambersburg PA
CBHW040122170426
42811CB00126B/1523